TAKING COVER

TAKING COVER

One Girl's Story of Growing Up During the Iranian Revolution

Nioucha Homayoonfar

Foreword by Firoozeh Dumas

NATIONAL GEOGRAPHIC

Washington, D.C.

Author's Note

To write my story, I relied upon my personal memories and those of my parents. I have changed the names of all of the individuals in this book, and in some cases, I modified details to protect loved ones.

Note About Language

The narrative includes a crude insult, the word "whore," which is used to frighten a teenage girl. This offensive word demonstrates part of the hostility the author experienced. It was included in the narrative to keep the authenticity of this true story.

Acknowledgments

My thanks to:

Lori Epstein, for taking a chance on her neighbor and handing my book proposal to the right people.

My wonderful editor, Martha E. Kendall, for her candid input and for always responding to my questions with so much patience and insight.

National Geographic, for providing me this platform.

Sheila M. Trask, for reading my story and telling me it had potential.

Everyone in my creative writing classes, and friends who read my manuscript and gave me their honest opinions about it.

My loving family.

Dedication

To Maman and Baba, for giving me these stories

To Sophie and Sawyer, the loves of my life

To Stew, for always being there

CONTENTS

FOREWORD

BY FIROOZEH DUMAS, BEST-SELLING AUTHOR OF *FUNNY IN FARSI*

High school was a pivotal time in my life, not for anything that happened at school, but for what happened on the other side of the world. Many evenings during my freshman year, I took my place on the sofa next to my parents as we watched the Iranian revolution unfold on the evening news. We lived in California, far away from the actual events, but we thought and spoke of nothing else. Still, if a fortune-teller had told us what the future held for Iran, we would have laughed in his face.

The Iran that we knew was a country with a cosmopolitan capital where women tried to emulate the latest European fashions, where the population was mostly secular, and where Jews, Christians, and Muslims co-existed peacefully. Women were making advancements in many fields, Iranian schools were producing world-renowned engineers and doctors, and more citizens than ever had access to educational opportunities.

Before 1979, most Iranians did not fathom that someday, women would no longer be allowed to serve as judges, that Western music would be banned, that women would be punished for showing strands of hair, that what happens socially in the privacy of your home, like dancing, could actually get you arrested. I still cannot believe that my favorite vacation spot as a child, the Caspian Sea, is now gender-segregated. How ridiculous is it that men and women can no longer enjoy the beach together?

Of course pre-revolutionary Iran had some very serious problems. We knew the shah's government was corrupt and knew the profit from oil, the country's main natural resource, did not go back to the people, but to the corrupt individuals with ties to the government. Members of the Bahá'í religion suffered for their beliefs. Iranians had little freedom of speech and the shah's critics were silenced.

With the overthrow of the shah, we, like many Iranians, were cautiously optimistic. We hoped that a non-traditional leader, someone who was not a politician, would herald a new era for Iran, an era of democracy and economic fairness. Ironically the overthrowing of the shah did not solve Iran's issues. The Iran of today has even more problems, and a society with far fewer rights.

Books like this, Nioucha Homayoonfar's *Taking Cover,* provide such an important and necessary window into the complexities of this country. Told from the point of view of a young French-Iranian girl coming of age in Iran, her story shows the changes, both big and small, that slowly became a way of life, forming the Iran that exists today. Her simple observations effectively yet powerfully illustrate how the Iran that she knew, the Iran that I knew, disappeared, bit by bit. Her descriptions of the changes in her school alone speak volumes about the opportunities afforded to Iran's youth before and after the revolution and why so many Iranians now live in exile. More important, her story shows us why those of us living in exile continue to love our culture and

our people, why we do our best to hang on to our memories, our language, our music, and our recipes.

Nioucha's colorful story will inevitably surprise many readers who do not visualize pre-revolutionary Tehran as a vibrant and international city, a city where John Travolta's dance moves were attempted by every teen with Saturday night fever and where the search for the latest and trendiest American tennis shoes was a serious venture. But there is an even more important reason to read *Taking Cover*. Even though readers will be entertained by Nioucha's memoir, I hope they will also ponder the vital underlying question: Can *my* freedoms be taken away? Does radical change always require a violent revolution or can rights be taken away slowly and silently?

I hope Nioucha's book will be discussed in schools, at home, and in book clubs across America. As Coretta Scott King so affectingly said, "Freedom is never really won. You earn it and win it in every generation."

—Firoozeh Dumas

Firoozeh Dumas is the author of the *New York Times* best sellers *Funny in Farsi* and *Laughing Without an Accent,* and the award-winning *It Ain't So Awful, Falafel*. She has also written articles for the *New York Times,* covering topics on her life as an Iranian-born woman raised in America. For more information, visit firoozehdumas.com.

FURY
1986 (PART 1)

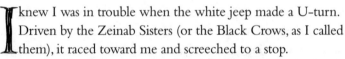

Javabe ablahan khamooshist.
—Persian proverb

Silence is the best answer to fools.

Iknew I was in trouble when the white jeep made a U-turn. Driven by the Zeinab Sisters (or the Black Crows, as I called them), it raced toward me and screeched to a stop.

My mother was pushing my little brother in a stroller. She had already crossed the street, but I'd lagged behind. So when the "Moral Police" pulled in front of me, I was all alone. Their job was to ensure that women and girls dressed in the manner dictated by Islam. To set an example, these four were covered head to toe in black chadors, and some of them even wore gloves.

The Black Crow sitting in the back seat jumped out and grabbed my arm without saying a word. I caught my mother's eye just as I was being pushed inside the jeep. Maman stood helplessly, screaming across the traffic for the Crows to let me go.

Alarmed by her yells and frantic gestures, a few passersby stared at the jeep. Through the window I saw my brother look up at Maman. His lower lip quivered, a sure sign he was about to cry.

The jeep just peeled away. "What is this?" Backseat Crow asked, pointing to my neck.

It was such a hot summer day that I had undone one of the top buttons of my navy robe. Wearing dark colors in the heat didn't help. A small triangle of neck showed, which of course they considered blasphemous. I automatically buttoned the top button and positioned my scarf to hide my neck.

"That's better," she said. "But what's this?"

My sleeves were rolled up a bit. She jabbed her finger toward the three inches of my arms that were exposed above my wrists. Clearly she believed that much flesh would be too much temptation for a man. I unrolled my sleeves.

"Haven't you girls learned anything yet?" Backseat Crow yelled. "How many times do we have to arrest you before you understand how to appear in public? What kind of a Muslim woman are you? Have you no modesty?"

The two front seat Crows sniggered. I lowered my eyes and folded my hands in my lap. I knew better than to argue. Getting hauled off in their car was a very bad sign. I wasn't about to worsen my situation by being the usual smart aleck I had been at school.

"We're about to teach you a lesson you won't soon forget," she continued. "Maybe then you'll respect the laws of Islam."

I nervously watched out the window to see where they were taking me. We drove by the man selling watermelons from his green pickup truck near Vanak Square. Baba often bought one from him on his way home from work. Pedestrians weaved through heavy traffic, and Driver Crow lay her hand on the horn like all the other drivers were doing. For me, this din from the street was nothing new, but I'd never heard such a roar in my ears as my blood was pulsing while my heart pounded.

"How old are you anyway?" Frontseat Crow said.

"I'm fifteen."

"It's time for you to be married," she said. "Otherwise, you'll get yourself in a lot of trouble. An insolent girl like you will soon bring shame to her family."

"Was that foreign-looking woman across the street your mother?" Driver Crow asked, glaring at me in the rearview mirror. "The one with the little boy in the stroller? Her scarf barely covered her blond hair."

"Yes. That was my mother."

The thought of Maman and Nima made me want to cry.

"Where is she from?" Driver Crow asked.

"She is from France."

"That explains it!" Backseat Crow said. "All Western women are whores. And you are the child of a whore. No wonder you prance around the streets baring your whole body for every man to see."

All the Crows laughed.

We reached Shahrak, a neighborhood where many houses and buildings were under construction. It couldn't have taken us more than 10 minutes to get there, but it felt like hours. I knew this area because my father had driven us around here. Baba thought it would be nice for our family to move to this developing part of Tehran.

The jeep turned into a deserted street with several cement trucks and cranes parked along the side. Driver Crow slowed down.

"Which one was it again?" she squawked.

"The brick one on the right, with the brown garage door."

We pulled into an apartment building garage. There were no other cars.

Backseat Crow pushed me out of the jeep and led me up one flight of stairs. The smell of fresh paint made me light-headed. The hallway windows still had adhesive tape to prevent the glass from shattering. It dawned on me that nobody was around, neither in this building nor in neighboring ones. Being midday, the construction workers must have been either napping at home or having lunch breaks off-site.

One of the Crows knocked on a door and a new Black Crow opened it.

"We have another one," Backseat Crow said. "Is the room free?"

"Yes."

Backseat Crow pulled me inside. The apartment was empty except for some white metal garden furniture in the center of the living room. The large window to the right of the doorway was covered with thick black curtains, slightly open at the center. It was so bright outside that the whole room was illuminated by that narrow slit.

My eyes scanned the room for any signs of torture devices. Nothing. I could smell tea from a samovar in the kitchen to the left. From behind, someone pushed me into one of the hard metal chairs. The same person then dug her hands into both my arms with such force that my fingers tingled from the lack of circulation.

Three Black Crows entered the living room and sat at the table. I didn't recognize any of them from the car. They must have already been in the apartment. Invisible Crow kept me pinned in place.

"What's your name?" Crow No. 1 asked.

"Nioucha."

"Nioucha?" Crow No. 2 repeated.

"Yes."

"Do you know what your name means?" she asked. Invisible Crow dug deeper into my arms.

"No."

I stared at the table. Of course I knew the meaning of my name, but I didn't want to have a conversation with them.

"'Nioucha' means someone who listens." I was surprised she knew this. Very few people knew the origin or meaning of my name. "Are you a good listener?"

"I try."

I barely recognized my own voice. The three Black Crows from the car entered the room.

14

"You should have seen how she was walking in the streets," Back-seat Crow said. She joined the others around the table. "Everything was out for the whole world to see!"

I stared harder at the table. My arms felt bloated, like a million ants had crawled under my skin and were struggling to find a way out.

"Don't you have anything to say for yourself?" Crow No. 1 said. I looked at her. I was surprised to see how pretty she was, especially her long eyelashes.

"No."

"What?" It was Frontseat Crow. "We can't hear you!"

"No, I don't." I tried to keep my voice steady.

"Let's lock her up for a while," Crow No. 2 said. "We'll decide later what to do with her."

"Wait!" I said.

"What?"

"Can I call my mother?"

"No."

"Please?"

"No! No calls are allowed," Backseat Crow said.

Invisible Crow released her grip on my arms. Instantly, the ants scattered. Crow No. 1 dragged my chair aside with such force that I was nearly flung forward. She punched my arm as a signal for me to get up. I did. She pushed me and I fell across the table. Everyone laughed.

"Put her in the back room," said Crow No. 2, the one with the really raspy voice. "I have someone else in the front room."

I pulled myself off the table. Backseat Crow took my wrist and yanked me to a room at the end of the hall. She opened the door and shoved me inside.

"Make yourself at home," she said.

She closed the door. I heard her lock it and remove the key. I glanced at my watch: 4:37 p.m. I rubbed my arms where I could

15

feel the fingernail indentations through my sleeves. I looked around the bare room. The walls were white, with dirty finger marks everywhere. Black curtains covered a small window, and a bare lightbulb hung from the ceiling. I pulled the curtains aside to discover that the window was barred. I tried to open it for some air, but it was sealed shut with tar. Looking out across the dirt road, all I could see was a building still under construction.

The room smelled of stale urine and sweat. The floor was carpeted, light gray with dark stains. I gagged. My legs almost gave way, but I didn't want to sit down and absorb a stranger's urine. I didn't even want to lean on the walls; the finger marks were disgusting. I hovered near the window, my hands in my pockets.

I thought about Maman, and immediately tears welled up in my eyes. I knew how sick with worry she must be. But I wasn't going to cry here. That's what they wanted, and I wouldn't give them the satisfaction. Those pathetic people. How could showing a bit of my neck and arm make me a whore?

What had happened to the Iran I had loved so much?

REVOLUTION
1979

Ze gahvare ta gur danesh bejooy
—Persian proverb

Seek knowledge from cradle to the grave

Everything started going wrong when I was eight years old. It wasn't just on the streets of Tehran, but also at home, with math homework—which, let me just say in plain language, I hated more than anything else in the world. I remember one day in particular when I sat at my desk, struggling and fuming over another impossible math problem. Maman kept trying to help me, but she was a math genius. I, for some lame reason, had not inherited that gene from her.

"Let's try this one more time," Maman said. "If Reza reads forty pages of his book in one day, how many pages has he read in five days?"

"I don't know," I said.

I was on the verge of tears from frustration and humiliation.

"It's a multiplication problem, right?" Maman said. "You need to multiply forty by … ?"

"I don't know."

"It's not as hard as you think, *chérie*," Maman said. "All right, let's start over. Now, if Reza …"

She was interrupted by loud banging noises, like fireworks.

Pop! Pop! Pop!

We ran to the living room to look outside.

"Get away from the windows right now!" Baba said, storming inside at that very moment. He must have left the radio station where he worked early. "There are mobs of people in the streets. It's a riot around Vanak Square."

"What?" Maman said. "So close?"

"What are they doing?" I asked. "What's a mob? What are those sounds?"

"There's no time! Hurry, over here." He motioned to the bathroom off the kitchen. "Get inside. We'll wait until the noise dies down."

Maman and I scurried into the bathroom. Seeing my father so nervous scared me more than all the sounds around us. He was talking to himself.

"There are no windows in the bathroom. We should be safe. Besides, we're on the third floor. I'm pretty sure gunshots can't reach that high up."

He rolled the kitchen's round table on its side and placed it in front of the bathroom to create a barricade. Then he closed the door.

We crouched under the bathroom sink and huddled in silence.

Pop! Pop! Pop!

"Baba, what's going on?" I asked.

"Shh, Nioucha, not now," Baba said.

I looked at Maman. She had squeezed her eyes shut as she held on to Baba's hand. I had no idea what was happening, but my heart slammed in my chest so hard I had to gulp for air.

I wondered if all this had anything to do with the man with epilepsy who had had a seizure right under our living room

18

window last week. Neighbors had run into the street to help him. Our landlord put a pencil in his mouth to stop him from biting his tongue. The landlord's wife put a pillow under his head so he wouldn't bang it against the pavement. I was terrified by the white foam coming out of his mouth and his eyes rolling back inside his head.

But these sounds had nothing to do with someone having an epileptic seizure. They seemed more serious and much scarier.

We heard a long series of loud bangs, some close, others far away. I kept straining my ears to gauge the distance of the racket.

From my vantage point under the sink, I counted 48 yellow tiles and 26 brown tiles going horizontally between the bathroom door and the shower. My eyes wide, I didn't blink.

After what felt like a long time, the noise died down. I relaxed into Baba's lap and began to doze off until Maman whispered to Baba, "What's going on out there?"

"I think this is IT for the shah."

Ah! Now the conversation I'd overheard at the party my parents hosted the week before began to make sense. Maman had sent me to bed, but I wasn't sleeping. I couldn't understand what I was hearing because people kept referring to "he" and I didn't know who "he" was. Now I knew they had meant the shah. The tension in everyone's voices had kept me glued to my door and awake long after I should have been asleep.

One of Baba's friends had said, "Everyone says he is corrupt and a puppet of the United States."

"People—his enemies—have been saying this for a long time," Baba said.

"But he's more unpopular than ever," the friend continued. "There are more and more demonstrations against him around the country. I think this is serious."

"It'll probably blow over," Baba had said. "Maybe he'll leave the country for a while, and wait until things settle down."

Remembering what I'd heard that night, I tried to keep still, pretending to be asleep in Baba's arms.

Maman said, "What do you think will happen now?"

A note of hysteria crept into her voice. I couldn't help stirring and opening my eyes. Baba shook his head, clasped me tighter against him, and said, "I'm not sure, but let's hope that was the end of it."

He stood up and opened the bathroom door. After listening for a few minutes, he said, "It stopped."

He rolled the table back to its place in the kitchen, but Maman and I still hadn't moved.

"Come on, my girls, it's over now."

We peeled ourselves out from under from the bathroom sink. Baba called family and friends to make sure they were safe. I sat in the TV room with Maman and Baba, afraid to stay alone in my room and trying to focus on my homework again. When Baba turned on the television, he drew his breath in and mopped his forehead with his handkerchief. I dropped my pencil and stared at the screen.

The news showed hundreds of people jamming the streets. On the screen, white smoke billowed and chants rang through the air, though I couldn't distinguish words. People milled around in the intersection. Then suddenly came the same loud bangs we'd heard in our apartment. The crowd panicked and ran in all directions. Then there was black smoke. I didn't recognize this area of Tehran. In the corner of the screen a van appeared, carrying soldiers with big guns. I began to feel nauseated from the jerky movement of the camera, but then Maman turned off the TV.

"It's past your bedtime," she said.

I went to bed, but I couldn't fall asleep. The sounds we'd heard, those scary bangs, kept ringing in my ears.

When Maman came in to kiss me good night, she said, "It's all right that you didn't finish your homework. That's completely understandable. I can write a note to your teacher if you want."

"Oh, I forgot I never finished it," I said.

"Well, it's been a … difficult day," she said. "Are you okay?"

"I guess so. But, what's going to happen?"

"I wish I knew, chérie. It's all a bit confusing right now."

"But I'm scared," I said.

"I'll stay with you until you fall asleep."

She hadn't done that in years, but I felt relieved to have her there with me.

The next day, most teachers, including mine, didn't come to school. With so few teachers present, the principal announced over the loudspeaker: "Good morning, children. Because of the unusual circumstances we find ourselves in today, so long as you behave yourselves, you are free to play games or study until your parents pick you up."

~

Hearing the principal's voice brought me back to my first day of school in Iran, three years earlier. I had stood outside my first-grade classroom crying, clutching Baba's hand and begging him not to leave. Dozens of children filled the courtyard and played under the large willow trees.

My new school was called Razi. It was for French-Iranian kids like me, or for Iranian kids who wanted to have a dual-language education. We had been given a tour of it when we came for registration. I couldn't believe my eyes. It was the biggest school I had ever seen.

Before moving to Iran we lived in Pittsburgh, Pennsylvania. At the time of my school tour we had been in Iran only a few weeks. Back in Pittsburgh, Baba had explained to me that he wanted to live near his family, that he missed his homeland. I was sad to leave the friends I had made in my preschool class. My preschool was in a room at the back of a church in our neighborhood.

By contrast, Razi had a large swimming pool, four tennis courts, a track field, a gymnasium, and a theater. The school was divided into several areas for preschool, kindergarten, elementary, middle, and high school. As soon as the bell rang, the children rushed into their classes, leaving Baba and me alone in the concrete hallway. With a gentle nudge toward the classroom, Baba said, "I'll wait right outside this door until recess, all right?"

"But I don't belong here!" I said.

"Nioucha, we've gone over this. You do belong here. Now go on."

Reluctantly, I picked up the schoolbag at my feet and flung it over my shoulder. Baba pulled out his handkerchief, the one he used for wiping his glasses and his balding head. Gently he dried my tears and runny nose, being careful not to drop the newspaper and book tucked under his left arm.

I sniffled deeply and gave Baba one last pleading glance. It had worked so well with him before, but not this time. He smiled, turned me around, and gave me a light but firm push. I walked into class and took my assigned seat in the front row.

Mrs. Darvish opened her large notebook and began roll call.

"Anahita A., Jean-Louis D., Bianca G."

She checked off names with a red marker and nodded curtly to each student after they called out, "Yes" in Persian, the language of Iran.

"Nioucha H.," she said.

I knew she was looking at me through her thick glasses, but I kept staring at my desk and fingering the strap of my schoolbag.

"Nioucha," she repeated, this time raising her voice.

I shared a school bench with Anahita. She elbowed me and whispered, "Say *baleh*."

I didn't want to.

Mrs. Darvish exhaled loudly and scribbled something in her notebook. When she finished calling everyone's name, she rose from her seat. She smoothed her pleated black skirt and turned it around to make sure the seams were placed properly on her ample hip bones.

She took a piece of blue chalk and said, "Is class ready for their lesson?"

She smiled and her glasses moved up against her forehead.

"Yes, Mrs. Darvish," the classroom answered.

She turned her back to us and began to write on the blackboard. All the kids in class took out their notebooks and pencils, ready to copy what the teacher wrote. Except me. I slipped my hands under my legs and rocked myself on the bench.

Anahita whispered, "Why aren't you doing anything?"

"Because I don't want to," I whispered back.

"But you'll get in trouble," she warned.

"Don't worry about me," I said.

She shrugged and returned to her notebook, her long braid swinging down her shoulder.

I glanced up and stared at the photo of the shah and his wife, Farah, displayed above the blackboard. They were the king and queen of Iran. In the picture, he wore a uniform with lots of medals, and she had on a gorgeous crown made of diamonds and pearls. They smiled down at us as if to say, "We are watching over you as you study."

I looked at the clock, wishing I knew how to read it. I understood Baba's digital watch because he'd taught me how it worked, but this one had the little arm and the big arm that confused me. I wondered how much longer it would be before the bell would ring and I could meet Baba. He hadn't started his job yet, but Maman had, so he was the one bringing me to school. The first two days I had cried so much that Mrs. Darvish had let me leave so I could sit with him just outside the classroom.

My eyes wandered to the posters by the door: rows of animals and fruits with the name next to each one. The animal poster had a picture of a yellow-and-blue canary, and I kept staring at him, willing him to fly out and sit on my finger like Titi, the canary I had in Pittsburgh, used to do.

Suddenly, Mrs. Darvish was standing directly in front of me.

"What are you waiting for?" she said. "Start working! You're supposed to practice writing *alef.*"

I followed her finger to where it pointed at the blackboard.

"Anahita," Mrs. Darvish said, "tell Nioucha about alef."

"Alef is the first letter of the alphabet," she answered.

"Very good," Mrs. Darvish said. Then to me, "So why aren't you working?"

"Because I'm not Iranian," I said. "I am French."

"You are both," Mrs. Darvish said. "And you are speaking Persian even though you're pretending not to understand me."

I sat staring straight ahead, thinking she'd eventually grow tired and walk back to her desk.

"Do you behave this way with Madame Martine in the afternoons too?" Mrs. Darvish continued.

"No," Anahita said. "Nioucha is a good student in Madame Martine's class."

Mrs. Darvish didn't like hearing this. Her eyebrows furrowed even more.

She leaned down, and through clenched teeth said, "Nioucha, if you don't start writing this minute, I'll break your hand."

Anahita gasped. I knew from how quiet the classroom grew that all the kids were staring at the teacher and me. My heart beat very fast and my cheeks felt warm. Before Mrs. Darvish could see my eyes getting teary, I looked down and slowly unzipped my schoolbag. I found my notebook and opened it to the first page. I reached in again, took out my pencil box, and chose the one with the pointiest tip.

Satisfied, Mrs. Darvish clapped her hands a few times and said, "All right, class. Keep practicing!"

She returned to her desk in the front of the room, where she stood and rifled through some papers. Anahita slipped her hand under her desk and reached for mine, giving it a firm squeeze.

I looked at her and she smiled.

Anahita was about to whisper something, but we heard Mrs. Darvish scraping her chair and sitting down. We let go of each other's hands. Mrs. Darvish looked around the classroom to make sure all students were working. I grabbed my pencil and pretended to be writing just as diligently as everyone else.

Finally, the bell rang for recess. I ran out as fast as I could. Baba was sitting on the low concrete wall that separated the courtyard from the soccer field. Bees flew around the yellow-and-purple pansies in the divider. When Baba noticed how flushed I was, he asked me what was wrong. I told him what had happened in class.

"I don't belong here, Baba," I said. The tears I'd been holding back through the class finally poured down my cheeks. "I don't want to go back ever again. The teacher said she'd break my hand!"

"Calm down, Nioucha," Baba said.

"But Mrs. Darvish is so mean to me," I said.

"Hold on, did you just say she threatened to break your hand?" Baba asked.

"Yes," I said.

"That's it. We're going to the principal's office right now."

"Can I come with you?" It was Anahita. She stood a few feet away from where we sat on the wall, but she must have heard our conversation.

I jumped up and took her hand. "Baba, this is Anahita. We sit next to each other in class. Her mother is French too. Can she come with us?"

"Hello, Anahita," Baba said. "Sure she can."

"I'll just walk with you a little ways," Anahita said.

We walked, still holding hands. Baba led the way to the high school part of Razi to reach the principal's office.

"You looked so sad in class," Anahita continued. "I wanted to see if you were okay."

"Thanks," I said. "I'm okay now."

I realized I wasn't crying anymore. Having Anahita there made me forget how miserable Mrs. Darvish had made me.

"Nioucha, why do you act like you don't know Persian?" Anahita said.

"I think …" I started. I dropped my voice, worried Baba might hear, even though he was walking pretty far ahead of us. "I think that if I am a bad student, Maman and Baba will take me back home to Pittsburgh."

She didn't say anything. So I asked, "Do you think they would?"

"I don't know. Maybe," Anahita said. "How did you learn Persian anyway?"

"Playing and watching TV with my cousins. We've been living at my aunt's house, and I am always hanging out with them."

"Okay," Anahita said. After a slight pause, she asked, "Do you have a Barbie?"

"I have two. Why?"

"I thought we could bring them to school and play during recess together. There's a clearing in the woods behind our building where we can play without anyone noticing. What do you think?"

"I think I'm bringing my Barbies to school tomorrow!" I said.

"Great! I'm going to go now, but I'll see you later."

"Okay, see you."

She ran back in the direction we'd come from. I turned around and stared at the yard ahead of me. It had a shallow pool decorated with turquoise tiles, and water flowed down to the next pool below, and the next and the next. It looked like a waterfall.

I caught up with Baba where he was waiting for me by a large limestone building. When we reached the principal's office, I remembered why we'd come, and my stomach squeezed. Baba asked the assistant for an immediate meeting. She nodded and, after a brief phone call, led Baba to a door and told me I had to wait outside. She gently put her hand behind my back and pointed to one of the chairs in the reception area.

A minute later, the principal burst out of his office and said to his assistant, "Ask Mrs. Darvish to come here straightaway. I need to speak with her." Then he turned to me and said, "Nioucha, come with me."

I followed him into his office. He was short and portly, with snow-white hair and a matching mustache. His office smelled of a pipe, the exact scent of the one Baba occasionally smoked.

We didn't have to wait long before Mrs. Darvish walked in. She adjusted her glasses and after nodding hello to Baba, took a seat next to him, across the desk from the principal. I sat behind Baba at a children's table strewn with books, coloring pages, and crayons. I absentmindedly picked up a green crayon to color in a frog sitting on a lotus leaf.

The principal relayed what he'd heard from Baba. He sounded angry and slammed his hand once on his desk.

"Mrs. Darvish, you know that this is not how we handle matters at Razi," he said. "I will not tolerate threats of violence toward a child. What came over you?"

"How dare you threaten to break my daughter's hand?" Baba said.

"I lost my temper," Mrs. Darvish said, "and I'm sorry." She looked down and fumbled with the pleats of her skirt. "But," she paused, "Nioucha refuses to do anything in class. It confuses the rest of the children."

"This child just moved here from America," the principal continued. "She is already juggling with speaking both English and French, and now she has a third language to deal with. Everything is new to her—the language, the culture, the people, everything. You need to be more patient with her."

"I will," Mrs. Darvish said.

"Nioucha needs some time to adjust, that's all," Baba said. "I'm sure that as soon as she begins to understand and speak Persian,

she'll be a very good student."

Mrs. Darvish turned around halfway in her seat and gave me a quizzical look. I felt heat rising in my face, realizing that now Baba would know my secret.

"But she already speaks Persian," Mrs. Darvish said.

"No, she doesn't!" Baba exclaimed.

"Mrs. Darvish, what are you talking about?" the principal asked.

"Well, every day Nioucha asks me what time it is and how much longer we have until recess."

The room fell silent. I continued coloring the leg of the frog, pretending not to notice the three of them staring at me.

In that moment I admitted to myself that I was not just visiting Iran. We lived here now. I wished the frog could pull me into his pond and magically whisk me back to Pittsburgh. Reluctantly, I glanced at Baba. He winked at me and smiled. So he wasn't angry with me after all. My head spun with relief and I ran into his arms. I whispered in his ear, "I promise I'll practice writing alef in my notebook tonight." Baba chuckled and squeezed me harder.

~

I giggled now, remembering what I had done three years ago when I pretended not to know Persian. Once I got used to it, I loved my school. But now no one knew what would happen next, and that made me worry. That night Baba walked into the living room and dropped a pile of newspapers on the coffee table. All of them read, "The Shah Left!" in large, bold letters. One had a picture of the shah and his wife, Farah, boarding an airplane. He'd been forced into exile.

Baba said, "I never thought I'd see the day."

I couldn't tell if he was glad or sad to see the shah go.

That night, I went to bed confused and stayed awake for hours. I heard Baba's animated voice rise and fall as he spoke to his friends on the phone or to Maman. I tossed and turned, and shook under my blanket until sleep finally released me.

ACTING
1980

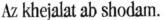

Az khejalat ab shodam.
—Persian proverb

I melted from shame.

The bell rang, signaling the end of recess. Anahita and I were running to the theater when we saw Keyvan squeezing his head through a thin slit in the metal gate. This gate used to separate the elementary and middle school from the high school, but now it separated the girls from the boys. Thin metal sheets had been hammered onto the gate so that kids on either side could not see each other. Now that the shah was gone, this new government was hard at work going against the progress the shah had wanted for his country. The new regime said it was against Islam for genders to mingle unless they were related by blood.

"Pssssst, psssst," he said.

"What is it?" I said.

"Come closer," he said. "I have something to tell you."

"We can get in trouble, Keyvan," Anahita said. "You're not supposed to be talking to us."

"Yeah, go away!" I said.

At least with our school no longer being coed, I didn't have to deal with Keyvan's annoying habits, like looking up my skirt or blowing me kisses during class. At nine years old, I knew what I didn't like—boys with annoying habits.

"But I want to tell you something," he continued.

"What is it?" I said.

"Have you heard about Bianca?" he said. "They've executed her father."

I gasped.

"Oh no!" Anahita said. She looked as if she might cry. I held on to her because my knees felt too weak to hold me.

"So that's why she hasn't been in school," I said. "Keyvan, how do you know this?"

"My uncle lives across the street from them. He said these men showed up late at night at Bianca's house, dragged her father out, and forced him in a car. Apparently, he was a general."

"This is so awful," I said. "It's so awful. Poor Bianca."

"What is she going to do?" Anahita asked.

"Don't know," Keyvan said. "Their house is completely dark. No lights on."

We stood there, shocked.

"Oh no, I gotta go!" Keyvan said.

He disappeared from the slit in the gate.

"Nioucha! We're waiting for you!"

It was our teacher, Mrs. Ganji, standing on the steps of the theater about 30 feet away. We must not have heard the bell ring because we were the only kids left on the playground.

"I'm coming! Sorry, Mrs. Ganji."

Anahita and I darted toward her, hoping Mrs. Ganji hadn't seen us talking to Keyvan.

I noticed Anahita wiping her eyes, and I paused.

"Anahita?"

She turned around, the rims of her eyes red.

"I can't believe Bianca's father's been killed," Anahita said.

I couldn't think of anything to say. It all seemed too much to even comprehend.

"I mean, we've heard about all these executions, right? But I didn't know anybody in person."

Anahita sniffed and dabbed her eyes. "Let's go, Nioucha."

"Are you sure?" I asked. "Do you need another minute?"

"Thanks, I'm good. Come on."

When we entered, our class was already getting into costume, rehearsing our upcoming play. I loved this theater. It could seat 150 people, and the walls were decorated with burgundy velvet. When I looked up, a giant gold sun smiled down at me, its rays extending out to the edges of the ceiling.

That's when I noticed that a large framed picture of Ayatollah Khomeini, our new leader, had been centered above the stage to replace the one of the shah and Farah. They had looked so friendly, smiling in their photo. But Khomeini frowned, and with his long white beard, he looked permanently angry. As a religious leader, he wore a turban.

From the minute he arrived in Tehran I hadn't liked him. He had turned our lives upside down. Now I saw him as something worse. As a killer. An executioner. I looked at that picture, willing him to notice me, but his eyes were downcast. He may have thought that he was a holy man and destined for heaven, but I had no doubt he was going to hell for giving the order to kill Bianca's father and dozens of other people whose only crime had been to serve a man that Khomeini despised.

"That's right," I thought, "don't meet my stare. The hatred in my eyes can surely burn a hole in your skull right now."

"Nioucha, get on stage and stop daydreaming," Mrs. Ganji said.

I snapped out of it and blinked. I had been so wrapped up in hating Khomeini that I couldn't remember what I was doing here. That morning, Mrs. Ganji had asked me to replace a classmate who

had gotten sick the night before.

"You'll play the part of the king's brother," Mrs. Ganji had said.

"I'm playing a boy?" I asked.

"Seeing as our school isn't coed anymore, yes, you are."

"But, Mrs. Ganji, I don't look like a boy."

"With a big turban and a fake mustache, you will. Now, let's rehearse."

A few months before, I had heard her say to another teacher, "Let's organize a play to keep the kids distracted from everything that's happening." I vaguely remembered Mrs. Ganji asking for volunteers to perform in a tale from *The Arabian Nights*. Most of the class had raised their hands high, nearly falling over their benches. Anahita had not, so even though I wanted to be in it, I didn't volunteer either. I didn't want her to feel left out. Later she told me she felt too shy to stand in front of a crowd, even if our performance was only going to be for students and a few teachers.

Now I understood her reluctance. In fact, I felt terrified to have been chosen. I tried to back out, but when Mrs. Ganji said I had no lines to memorize, I agreed to do it. My part as the king's brother was to sit next to him and eat what the servants presented on trays.

That seemed simple enough, and I did well during rehearsal just sitting there on my chair and pretending to eat invisible cookies. The following day after our lunch break, the entire elementary school filed into the auditorium for our performance. I was all dressed up in a green velvet robe and sat proudly onstage. At one point in the play, a servant brought a platter of raisin cookies and I ate two, careful not to get any crumbs on my fancy outfit. During the rehearsal, the tray had been empty, so this was a nice surprise. Before I knew it, the play ended with tremendous applause from the packed auditorium. I felt a little embarrassed to bow my thanks along with all my classmates because I knew I hadn't done anything to deserve such a warm reception.

Backstage, Mrs. Ganji greeted us with hugs and kisses. She then asked us to line up behind the curtain and get ready to return to the stage, introduce ourselves, and say what part we played.

I was the first to go, except I didn't know what I was supposed to say. All this time I'd thought I had *no lines,* and now faced with this new piece of information, I stood completely frozen. Mrs. Ganji must have noticed the panic in my eyes because she took my hand and said, "Nioucha, don't be scared. Just go out there, say your name, and the role you played."

"And how do I do that?"

"Well, you take the microphone and say 'Nioucha H. in the role of the prince.'"

I couldn't feel my tongue. My ears were warm and made strange noises. I walked onstage and stared out into the crowd as I held the microphone to my mouth. My heart was pounding furiously. I couldn't remember what I had to say. I looked back to Mrs. Ganji for help, but she only motioned for me to hurry up.

"Hi! I am the prince playing the role of Nioucha H."

With all the buzzing in my ears, I barely heard my own voice. I glanced over at Mrs. Ganji, pleased to have gotten words out of my mouth. When I looked back at the audience to bow, I saw that everyone was laughing. Anahita covered her mouth to hide the fact that she wanted to laugh too.

She winked, waved with her other hand, and shrugged as if to say, "It's no big deal."

Mrs. Ganji came out, took the microphone from me, and looking very amused, whispered, "It's all right, Nioucha. At least everyone will remember you now."

I returned backstage and hid in the dressing room until it was time to go home. When I thought most of the school had emptied, I ran out to meet Baba, who was picking me up. Baba asked about the play, but I refused to answer him at first, not wanting to relive the shameful experience. But then he gave me his coaxing look and his wink, and I relented. When I finished, I glanced over and caught him smiling.

"It's not funny, Baba," I said a little too loudly. "Everyone was laughing at me!"

"It's a little funny."

He reached across the gearshift and gently pinched my cheek. "Try to see the humor in it and laugh along with your friends."

I couldn't let my embarrassment go. And then I felt worse than embarrassed. I felt ashamed that I'd been so caught up in the play that I'd forgotten about Bianca and her father.

"Baba, I have something to tell you."

I told him what Keyvan had said. Baba drove quietly for so long that I finally asked, "Did you hear me?"

"I did. I'm sorry about your friend and her father."

His lips were very thin, like they got when he was angry or concentrating on something. His hands gripped the wheel hard, turning his knuckles white. I didn't know what to say or do, so I slouched inside my collar and closed my eyes. I soon realized we weren't on our way home.

"Where are we going?" I asked.

"To Minoo's."

When we reached my aunt's house, Baba rushed up the driveway. I followed him inside. After exchanging greetings, he leaned into his sister's ear and whispered something. She turned pale and slapped her cheek with her hand in despair. It wasn't the first time I'd seen her or other Iranians do this, but it still took me by surprise that someone would actually hit their own face to show how shocked they were about something. Aunt Minoo's legs seemed to sway under her, so Baba held her arm. They walked briskly into the library, closing the door behind them.

I stood awhile in the entrance of Aunt Minoo's house, waiting for them to come out. But they didn't. Eventually, I walked into the kitchen and looked around the room. This house was so familiar to me, it felt like my second home. Minoo was only two years younger than Baba, and they had been very close growing up. When we had moved to Iran from the United States, we lived with Minoo and her family for almost six months before finding our own apartment.

~

That first night in Tehran, Aunt Minoo's house had looked like a castle I might have seen in a cartoon. With all the lights on and situated on top of a hill, her home glowed in the dark almost like a Halloween jack-o'-lantern. There was a beautiful smell in the air, one I had not known before. Two large jasmine bushes stood on either side of the entrance, filling the evening with their magical perfume.

Aunt Minoo had given us a tour of their new two-story house. She was so excited to show it to us. Every room had bright colors. The living room and dining room were decorated in white curtains and Persian rugs, with tall windows all around. The kitchen had maroon tiles and white cabinets. Large wooden bookcases lined the library walls, and an inviting brown leather sofa waited for anyone who wanted to sit and sample any of the books. Upstairs, my cousin Sara's room was all pink, my cousin Omid's room was brown and orange, my aunt and uncle's room was all white, the guest bedroom was orange, and the TV room was beige. I felt like I'd walked into a rainbow.

When Aunt Minoo spoke, it sounded like she was laughing. She was petite, but her big smile looked like Baba's. I had overheard Baba say to Maman how happy he was that his sister had married well, affording her luxuries the rest of the family did not have. He said she was the most generous person he knew and that she loved to share her wealth with those around her.

Sara took after her mother in her generosity and kind spirit. Already 14 when we arrived, she shared her bedroom with me, her five-year-old cousin.

She had arranged her collection of stuffed animals neatly on her dresser—a dozen cats, five puppies, and three frogs. I really liked

the frogs. I'd never seen any at the toy store Maman used to take me to in Pittsburgh. I had been surprised to see that a teenager still had toys in her room, but I had instantly loved her for it.

Despite feeling comfortable with my cousin, I felt scared in Aunt Minoo's big house.

One morning, just a few weeks after we came to Iran, Maman had pulled the pink curtains aside in Sara's room to let the sun in. Maman wore a short-sleeved navy dress with a red belt, and a wide red headband held back her long blond hair. She looked normal to me, but something about the house felt far from normal.

"Good morning, chérie."

"Good morning, Maman. Can you come to the bathroom with me?"

"Are you still frightened?" Maman asked.

"Maman, there's a ghost living outside that bathroom window. I just know it."

"All you're hearing is the ivy from the neighbor's house rustling in the breeze."

"No, Maman, I've heard the ghost walking. It is really scary."

"I'm sure it's just the neighbor's cat walking on the gravel downstairs. You've seen that cat. He's adorable."

"It's not the cat."

"All right, Nioucha. It's time for me to go now."

"Are you leaving already?"

Maman had started working for a French oil company as an executive secretary.

"Yes, I'm leaving soon," she said, kissing the top of my head.

I wrapped my arms around her waist, wishing she could stay longer, at least through breakfast.

"Can't you take me to school today?" I asked.

"I'm sorry, chérie, but I can't."

This was the first job Maman had taken since I was born, and I couldn't stand not having her all to myself anymore.

When I wouldn't let go, she added, "I'll be here when you get

back from school. I have to go now. Baba will take you."

One more kiss and she was gone.

It seemed to me that Maman and Baba were hardly around anymore. They were always invited to parties with Aunt Minoo and her husband, and they left me with Sara and her 11-year-old brother, Omid. I remembered what had happened the night before, and I ran after Maman.

"Wait, Maman!"

She was halfway down the stairs. I ran into her arms and buried my face in her belly again.

"What's wrong?" she asked.

"You'll be back, right?"

"Of course I will."

"Promise?"

"I promise."

The night before, I had whimpered in Sara's lap, asking her over and over when Maman and Baba would be back.

"I'll go make us some dessert," Sara said. "That'll cheer you up."

She left me in the TV room with Omid.

As soon as she was downstairs in the kitchen, Omid said, "Your parents abandoned you. They're never coming back."

"That's not true," I said.

"Sure it is," Omid said. "They told me so."

He left the room and returned with my toy telephone. He dropped it in my lap.

"Here," he said. "Call them yourself and ask."

I started dialing a number.

"Maman? Hello? Hello?"

Of course, nobody answered. Omid sat in front of me and sneered. I couldn't stop myself from crying.

"What's going on?" Sara asked when she returned, holding a tray with three ice cream bowls. She put the desserts down on the coffee table and knelt beside me.

"Maman and Baba left me forever!" I wailed. "Omid said they're never coming back! Hello? Maman?"

I still held the telephone receiver to my ear. Omid laughed. Sara pushed her brother and he tumbled sideways.

"Get out of here," Sara said. "What's wrong with you?"

Sara pulled me into her lap and rocked me.

"Your mom and dad are with my mom and dad at a friend's house," Sara said. "I promise they haven't left you. Don't listen to Omid. He doesn't know what he's talking about."

Omid had taken one of the ice-cream bowls and gone to his room, slamming the door.

After he'd been so mean to me the night before, I dreaded having to see him again at breakfast.

I gave Maman one last squeeze before she left for work. Then I slowly made my way down the semicircular staircase to join the family in the kitchen.

Aunt Minoo stood by the stove making scrambled eggs while Sara and Omid sat at the table drinking fresh-squeezed orange juice. My aunt already had feta cheese, butter, walnuts, and quince jam on the table. The samovar brewed tea on the white kitchen counter. Through the large bay window, I saw Baba sitting in the garden reading the newspaper.

"Good morning," I said.

Aunt Minoo turned around and blew me a kiss.

"Good morning, sleepy girl," Sara said. She patted the chair next to her. I took a seat, linking my arm through hers, making sure I avoided looking at Omid. Meanwhile, he rolled his eyes upward and stuck his tongue out. Sara kicked him under the table and he yelped.

"What happened?" Aunt Minoo asked Sara.

"He did the eye and tongue thing again," Sara said.

My aunt served us each large spoonfuls of eggs.

"Omid, what did I tell you about being nice to Nioucha?" Aunt Minoo said. "She is our guest. Treat her like a sister."

"But I already have a sister," Omid said. "I don't want another one!"

"You will do as I say," Aunt Minoo said. "And you will apologize."

Omid dropped his gaze and mumbled, "Sorry."

"Okay," I said.

Aunt Minoo sat to my left, cupped my chin, and kissed me on the cheek. I loved her round face, button nose, dark brown hair, and big green eyes. Her kids had her features, except their eyes were the color of milk chocolate.

Aunt Minoo served herself a tall glass of piping hot tea and began to drink. I played with my food while Sara and Omid ate.

Aunt Minoo said to me, "Have a few bites. It'll give you energy for school."

I picked up a piece of *barbari* bread, a thick Iranian flatbread with sesame seeds sprinkled on top. It was still warm. Since we'd arrived here, Baba had made it his mission to get fresh bread every morning for the family. He had missed Iran a lot in the 13 years he'd lived away from it.

"I'm not hungry yet," I said.

"You take after your father, then," Aunt Minoo said.

"Really?"

"Oh yes. You remind me of him when he was a boy."

She gazed out the window, looking adoringly at Baba.

"I'm so happy you moved to Tehran," Aunt Minoo continued. "I missed the first few years of your life but I hope to make it up to you now."

~

That sense of comfort and peace I had felt three years ago was long gone now. After Baba and Aunt Minoo had gone into the library, both looking really distressed, I sat alone in the kitchen until Sara joined me. We were quiet. All I heard was our deep breathing. Then Sara and I looked at each other, and without saying a word, we crept up to the library door and positioned our heads against it.

"Then where is he?" Aunt Minoo said. "Where is our uncle?"

Her voice was squeaky.

"I think he's gone into hiding," Baba answered.

Sara and I stared at each other. They were talking about their uncle, my grandfather Agha Jan's brother, who'd been a minister for the shah.

"Does anyone know where he is?" Aunt Minoo asked.

"No."

"Do you think he could be in prison?" Aunt Minoo asked.

"I don't know, sister."

Baba sounded so tired.

"What's happened to him, then?" Aunt Minoo asked.

"Sister, all I know is, if he'd been executed, his name would have been released in the newspapers."

I shivered, hearing that word: executed. Bianca's father, executed.

We heard muffled cries. Baba spoke to his sister in a hushed tone, making it impossible for us to distinguish any more words. After a long while, Baba walked out of the library and bumped into Sara.

"Girls, don't stand here," he said. "Go do your homework."

Sara took my hand and led me back to the kitchen. She fixed me a plate of barbari bread, butter, and feta cheese, my favorite afternoon snack. Sara poured herself a tea from the samovar and we sat at the table.

"Sara, do you think Great-Uncle has gone into hiding? Or have they … has something bad happened to him?"

"I don't know." Then after a long pause she said, "Maybe we should let the adults worry about these things."

I knew Sara was trying to be comforting. My hands shook when I tried to spread butter on my piece of bread. Baba's troubled face and Aunt Minoo's tearful voice rattled around my head. It was hard not to worry when our world was changing in ways we could not control. What might come next?

RETREAT

SUMMER 1980

Ghatre daryast, agar ba daryast
varna ghatre ghatre, darya daryast
—Persian proverb

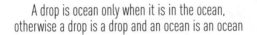

A drop is ocean only when it is in the ocean,
otherwise a drop is a drop and an ocean is an ocean

Aunt Minoo phoned one afternoon early in the summer, and Baba smiled when he hung up. He told us, "I think we could all use a break from what's been going on in Tehran. Minoo has suggested we go to Shomal for some peace and quiet."

My parents and Aunt Minoo's family rented a cottage there. It had its own small private beach. We were going to vacation for a week.

I really wanted my grandmother, Maman Bozorg, to come too, but she said she didn't like the north's damp air.

We drove to Shomal in two cars. When we reached the winding road of Chaloos, I started feeling sick. I felt embarrassed that I still got carsick at nine years old. I lay down in the backseat so I could fall asleep and avoid an upset stomach. My strategy worked. When I woke up we were almost there. Maman was guiding Baba with directions she'd written in her notepad.

"We're looking for number fourteen," she said. "It should be on the left."

"Here it is," Baba said as he slowed down and pulled into a driveway. I saw a little house to the left of the entrance and wondered if this was the cottage. It looked so small.

"This must be the gardener's house," Maman said. "He lives here all year with his family."

We drove down a long dirt road lined with tall trees until we reached the cottage, a plain cement structure built on a raised platform. A terrace ran the length of the house, facing a garden that led to the beach.

I jumped out of the car, happy to stretch my legs. It was warm, but unlike what everyone said about Shomal's weather, it was not humid. The air smelled like the sea. As we walked toward the cottage, we heard someone greet us from behind.

"Welcome," he said. "I am the gardener. I've been expecting you."

He led us to the cottage and gave us a tour. Sara and I ran ahead of the group, opening all the doors and inspecting all the closets. I liked the wooden furniture and paneling. The three bedrooms were all nearly identical with four simple twin beds in each. The living and dining areas were combined in one large square room containing a brown sofa and a long table with 10 chairs around it. White tiles covered the floors, with no rugs or carpets. I had grown so accustomed to seeing Persian carpets in every home that I liked the cool sparseness of this place.

In order to get to the kitchen, we had to exit the living room through a large sliding glass door and enter the kitchen through a separate door. It was strange that there was no direct access to it from inside the cottage. I ran back to Maman and said, "I wish we could live here forever." The gardener laughed and said, "God willing, the cottage will be here for decades to come. This place was built in the 1960s, and since then the Caspian has been rising. The owners are afraid that the garden might soon be submerged. But never mind that now, let me show you the rest of the property."

We followed along behind him, but on the steps down to the garden, I stopped. Dozens of snails covered this wall of the cottage, which was crisscrossed with their tracks. Sara joined me.

"Look at all these snails," I said.

"They're gross," Sara said. "We should get rid of them."

She stepped inside the cottage and returned with two big plastic pails.

"Let's pry them off and throw them in the buckets," she said.

We set to work.

"You're wasting your time with those snails," the gardener said as he passed us, leading the group back into the house.

"But I don't want them to come inside," Sara said.

"They won't," the gardener said. "You don't need to worry."

"We'll dump out the buckets far away from the cottage to be sure they don't come back," Sara said.

"The only way to get rid of those is to drown them in soapy water," the gardener said. "Do you want to hand me those buckets?"

"No, no," Sara said. "There's no need to do that."

"Very well," the gardener said.

Sara and I emptied the buckets near the tennis court, but when we turned around the snails immediately started making their way back to the cottage, leaving slimy trails in their wake.

~

Each morning, I helped Aunt Minoo purchase fresh food for the day while everyone else slept. Our cottage was a 20-minute drive from the nearest town, Noshahr. On our way to Noshahr, the mountains stood to our left, the Caspian Sea to our right. According to some locals, numerous *mojahedin* were taking refuge in these green, lush mountains.

I brought my binoculars, hoping to spot hidden *mojaheds*. But Aunt Minoo liked to keep reminding me that "the mountain's green thicket is impenetrable." She also said that these mojaheds were "a bunch of crazy leftist Islamist students who were opposed to both the shah and Ayatollah Khomeini." At nine years old, I had no idea what that meant. All I knew was that I hoped to see one of them hiding in the jungles like wild animals.

When we arrived in Noshahr, Aunt Minoo parked the car near the central shopping area shaped in a semicircle around a city square. The first thing I noticed as we walked toward the market was the smell of dust washed away with water. A few merchants were hosing the front of their shops, careful not to get us wet, and then they swept their storefronts clean, beckoning us in with *"Befarmaeed"* or "Please come in." The second thing I noticed was that unlike Tehran, Noshahr had quiet, uncrowded streets.

Aunt Minoo accepted the invitation of a fruit merchant and stepped into his shop.

"What are these?" she asked the fruit salesman, holding a bunch of grapes at arm's length. Even through her large, dark sunglasses, he could see how appalled she was that he was trying to sell such bad fruit. In Iran, it was customary to argue with salespeople about the quality of their products.

"They're good grapes. What do you think they are?"

"Give me your best fruit from the back," she said, dropping the grapes. "You think I'm going to buy this fruit?"

"What's wrong with it?"

Turning from the grapes to the cherries, she said, "Look at these, they're small and rotting. Don't you have anything better in the back?"

"This is all I have. Take it or leave it."

Maman and Baba, after having lived abroad, rarely bargained, but I was fascinated with Aunt Minoo's strong attitude. She was normally all smiles, but for the first time I saw that when she shops, she was transformed into a bull.

"Let's go to another fruit vendor, Nioucha," Aunt Minoo said,

gently pushing me out of the store.

"Be my guest!" the fruit salesman shouted after us.

We walked to the grocer next door. The same routine followed, until the vendor brought her his best fruit from the back, where he saved it for his preferred customers. Next on our list was the butcher. Aunt Minoo wanted to buy three pounds of lamb for a stew and two chickens for a salad.

"This meat smells," she said, handing back to the butcher the cubes of meat laid out on a piece of paper. "It's not fresh enough. Do you have anything better in the back?"

"My man just brought me this lamb this morning," the butcher said. "It doesn't get any fresher than this."

"Come on, I know good meat from bad."

"This is all I have. Take it or leave it."

She left it. The butcher next door sold the meat that smelled to her liking. He became our butcher. Aunt Minoo couldn't find anything wrong with the baker's fresh bread, so we bought a dozen flatbreads.

Mingled with the aroma of bread was the pungent smell of pick-led garlic. Most of the stores carried large jars of garlic as well as buckets with a ladle, the full cloves marinating in vinegar. I stopped to look at one, admiring the perfect shape of each bulb while some-what repelled by their strong odor.

"Would you like some?" Aunt Minoo asked.

"No thanks."

"They're a specialty of Shomal. They're really good for you."

"Maybe another time. I don't like their smell."

Aunt Minoo laughed. With all our shopping done and the sun beginning to warm up, I helped her carry the provisions to the car. I knew Aunt Minoo, an excellent cook, would make something delicious with whatever we bought.

Maman felt the same about Aunt Minoo's cooking. One day she asked Aunt Minoo to make a *ghormeh sabzi*. She knew that this had become my favorite stew. While Sara and I sipped cantaloupe juice on the terrace just outside the kitchen, we watched our mothers standing at the counter.

Aunt Minoo washed bunches of parsley, coriander, and green onions over a large sieve. After she dried them, she finely chopped all the herbs.

"How much parsley did you have there?" Maman asked. She held a pad and pen, set to take thorough notes.

"I'm not sure. Two handfuls?" Aunt Minoo replied.

Maman wrote in her pad. Always a stickler for details, she tried to hide her frustration that there wasn't an exact amount.

Then she watched Aunt Minoo chop up a large onion and sauté it in a skillet. Maman took note of that. Once the onion began to brown, Aunt Minoo took a jar of turmeric and poured some over the onions.

Aunt Minoo proceeded to sauté the lamb cubes with the onions. When they had browned, she took the pot to the faucet and poured water into it. The aroma lured me from the terrace and into the kitchen so I could peer into the pot.

Aunt Minoo brought the pot back to the stove, added red kidney beans, and seasoned the growing creation with salt and pepper, lemon juice, and a handful of limes. Then she sautéed the chopped herbs in a skillet until they looked dark green and crispy.

"Was that a tablespoon of lemon juice?" Maman asked. "How many cups of kidney beans did you add?"

"I don't know, Michelle. I'm too used to eyeballing my cooking." Aunt Minoo sounded apologetic. "Simply throw in everything like I just did and I'm sure your ghormeh sabzi will be delicious."

Maman shut her notepad, her French need for exact instructions unsatisfied. But she smiled and thanked her sister-in-law for her help.

I loved Aunt Minoo's meals, but my favorite activity at Shomal was not eating. It was swimming. Sara and I liked to swim far out into the sea. When everyone on the beach looked like a dot to us,

the water became so clear that we could see our legs and feet.

Ali, the gardener's son, sometimes joined us on his pedal boat. I pretended not to notice Ali and Sara flirting. I liked Ali because he brought us bologna sandwiches and bottles of Coca-Cola. Ali liked Sara because she laughed at his silly jokes. While they bantered back and forth, she twirled her long hair around her finger.

Omid didn't like swimming in the Caspian. He didn't even like being at Shomal. If somebody asked him what was wrong, he yelled that he'd much rather be back in Tehran hanging out with his friends and listening to Pink Floyd music.

I decided it was time to set Omid straight and get some revenge for the way he'd tormented me when I first came to Iran. I asked him 10 times a day to join Sara and me in the sea, knowing he didn't want to. He claimed the waves prevented him from swimming like he would in the upcoming competitions in Tehran. He said he should only swim in the pool to preserve proper form. Because he'd won four years in a row, he didn't want to jinx his luck now. But I kept nagging him.

Then, one morning on the way to the beach I told him, "I think you are a terrible swimmer if you can't even swim in the sea. I bet your trophies are fake."

Omid's round cheeks flushed. For a moment, I thought he was going to lunge at me. Instead, he darted inside the cottage and then emerged wearing his red-and-black bathing suit. He ran ahead of me, dove headfirst in the sea, and swam the butterfly— his specialty—for a few minutes before I joined him in the water.

Schools of small silver fish swirled around us. I noticed some dead ones floating nearby as well. This gave me an idea.

I challenged Omid to try swimming underwater and passing between my legs without coming into contact with them. I taunted him, "I have perfected this maneuver. You don't stand a chance."

"Fine, I'll play."

"Great! Let's see what you can do," I said.

"You play such dumb games," he scoffed.

I let Omid begin. When it was my turn, Omid moved farther out to make it more difficult for me to stay underwater. He seemed to have forgotten that family and friends had nicknamed me "the duck" because I loved being in the water so much.

I took a deep breath. On my way to Omid's parted legs, I snatched a dead fish. As I swam underneath him, I pulled his bathing suit and threw the dead fish inside. I passed through his legs and came up behind him.

"It's your turn, Omid!" I yelled.

At first, he didn't realize what I'd done. He simply asked, "Why did you touch my bathing suit?"

But when he saw me bobbing above the waves, grinning from ear to ear, he got suspicious. He felt his suit and then swam frantically to the shore. When he found the dead fish, he jumped up and down, screaming, "Get it away from me! Get it off of me!"

Watching him bounce hysterically, his wet, curly hair flying all around him and sticking to his face, made me laugh so hard that I swallowed mouthfuls of seawater. But it was worth it.

~

During one of the many beautiful afternoons when the weather was perfect, dry and sunny, Sara became restless and asked if I wanted to go for a drive around Noshahr with her. Of course I did! At 18, she had just gotten her driver's license. Both sets of parents hesitated briefly, but when they saw our faces, they gave in, making us promise to return in two hours. Sara and I ran inside to change our clothes. I threw on a T-shirt and shorts over my bathing suit and slipped on my plastic flip-flops. Sara put on a pretty blue summer dress.

Baba and Omid played backgammon on the terrace.

"Omid, will you come with us?" Sara asked him in a hushed tone.

"What for?"

"To be with me when I drive," she said.

Sara didn't feel comfortable driving yet. She still had a hard time shifting gears. Even though Omid was only 15 and too young to drive legally, he had taken the wheel when he and his dad ran errands in the neighborhood. For him, driving seemed easy.

"No, I'm not coming," he told Sara. "I hate being around you girls all the time. But can you buy me a soccer ball? I want to play with Ali and his friends."

"No," Sara said. She hit him hard on the arm and stalked off. I stared at him while he rubbed his arm, pleased to have witnessed his older sister angry with him. He noticed me standing there. "Boo," he yelled. I jumped and ran after Sara.

We took off in Aunt Minoo's brown Toyota. With the windows down we sped down the open road and sang along with Googoosh. I reached to turn the music louder, but Sara grabbed my arm.

"We can't play the music too loudly," she said.

"Why?"

"Because music is banned now," Sara said.

"It is? Since when?"

"A few months ago. We can't listen to any Western music or Iranian music from before the revolution."

"But what about all the new chants we've been hearing on the radio and television?"

"That's different. That's *their* propaganda music."

"Oh."

"Yeah. Classical music and traditional Persian music are okay too."

"What would happen if they heard us playing Googoosh?"

"Hmmm, not sure. Maybe the revolutionary guards would confiscate my cassette? Or give us a warning not to listen to it again?"

"Okay, I'll keep a lookout for any guards."

"I haven't seen any since we got here. I'm not too worried."

"Sara, remember when we went to Googoosh's concert?"

"How can I forget? She was amazing."

"And do you remember my Googoosh haircut?"

"I sure do. It looked so nice on you."

~

Two years before, Sara had gotten my parents' permission to take me to a Googoosh concert. My parents were reluctant at first, because I was only seven, but they relented after hearing Sara say, "Googoosh is the most beautiful and talented singer in Iran." We were all going: my family, Sara's family, and Maman Bozorg.

The only other singers I knew of before Googoosh were Donny and Marie Osmond. Since I was in love with Donny and was certain I would marry him when I grew up, I purposely forgot about Marie. But when I saw Googoosh on *Rangarang,* Iran's weekly entertainment show, I stared hard at the television. I loved her every move and wanted to imitate everything she did.

The day of the concert, Aunt Minoo hired a hairdresser to come to her house to cut or dye everyone's hair. My aunt's large bedroom suite turned into a salon.

When it was my turn, the hairdresser asked me what I wanted. My hair was so long it almost covered my whole back. In a sudden flash I said, "Cut it short like Googoosh's. I love her hairstyle."

"Which one?" he asked. "That woman must have a closet full of wigs. Every day she has a different one."

"No way," Sara said. "Her hair is all natural. I've seen it."

"Me too," I said.

"If you say so, ladies," the hairdresser said. "Nioucha, which style do you want?"

I glanced over at Maman for her approval. She had recently said that my hair had gotten too long to manage. I figured she wouldn't mind. When I saw her smiling, I turned around and said, "I want the one with the part down the middle and layers on both sides."

"The one with the length a little below the ears?"

"Yes, that's the one."

The hairdresser grabbed my long ponytail and in one swift motion,

cut it right off and put it on the dresser before me. I gasped. There was my wavy tail. For as long as I could remember my hair had been long. I began to feel like I had made a huge mistake, asking for such a drastic change instead of my usual trim. Just as the scissors came near my head again, I cringed and sank deep into the chair.

Straightening my head, the hairdresser said, "What's wrong? I hope you didn't change your mind."

"No ... I mean, yes, maybe, a little," I said.

"Give me a few minutes," he said. "I know you're going to love your new look." He confidently set to work.

After blow-drying my hair, he held up a mirror. I looked just like Googoosh.

"Do you like it?" the hairdresser asked.

I felt so relieved that I couldn't stop smiling at my reflection.

"I love it," I said.

"You look like a big girl," Sara said.

"Your hair looks wonderful," Maman said.

Maman Bozorg brought an empty shoebox she found in Aunt Minoo's walk-in closet, wrapped up the ponytail that had been cut off in a sheet of newspaper, and placed it in the box.

"You should keep your hair, my child," she said.

"What for?" I didn't like the thought of keeping my dead hair.

"As a keepsake of your youth."

I looked at her for further explanation, but she walked into the bathroom to wash the brown dye out of her hair.

That night, we had front-row tickets to the concert at the Hilton Hotel in Tehran. Googoosh was even prettier in person. Her silver dress sparkled when she danced. She sang all the songs I liked and at one point she looked directly at me and winked. I thought I'd burst with excitement. As she danced, one of her clip-on earrings fell down her dress. Googoosh said, "Oops" and wiggled to let it slide, then scooped down, picked it up, and put it back on. Only she could make a stage goof-up look so charming.

For weeks after seeing Googoosh in person, I played her music in Sara's room. Sara and I tried to remember everything she had done onstage so we could dance just like her.

~

Now I wished Sara and I could listen to Googoosh loudly in the car. But we couldn't do that anymore. Sara drove slowly and carefully. Her gentle speed allowed me time to look for both mojaheds and revolutionary guards with my binoculars. Between the cottage and Noshahr, ours was the only vehicle on the road, but once we arrived in Noshahr's small shopping center, Sara grew nervous. Even though there were only a few cars, it took her eight attempts to park in a spot that could have easily fit three cars. I pretended not to notice because I knew how sensitive Sara was about her driving. When she'd parked, I congratulated her on doing such a fine job. She smiled and said, "Let's find a pay phone."

"What for?" I asked.

"To call my boyfriend. I haven't spoken to him in four days and I really miss him."

On the next block stood a phone booth, with two people already in line. We kept walking along the main street where I had done the shopping with Aunt Minoo until we reached another pay phone.

"Why don't you buy *koloochehs* from that man down there?" Sara said, pointing to a street vendor farther down the block. "I'll meet you there in a few minutes."

Maman had given us money to buy these soft cookies with their delicious walnut filling. They were a specialty of Shomal, and I'd been eating nearly a dozen of them a day since we'd gotten here. And each was larger than the palm of my hand!

I bought eight boxes of koloochehs. Each box contained four plastic-wrapped cookies. Sara joined me a few minutes later, all smiles and bounciness.

"Let's buy a cake for everyone," she said.

"I haven't seen a bakery around here," I said.

"Fine, then let's buy Omid a soccer ball," Sara said. "I feel bad about hitting him."

At the general store, at least a dozen soccer balls hung from their net bags on a pole outside. We bought Omid a ball. We strolled back to the car, walking by the fruit vendor with his large platters of cherries, grapes, watermelons, and cantaloupes. The air smelled so sweet.

"Sara, I didn't know you had a boyfriend."

"It's new," Sara said.

"Are you going to marry him?" I asked.

"What? No! I don't know. I just met him two weeks ago."

"Do you love him?" I asked.

"I think I'm getting there. Tell you what, when we return to Tehran, I'll introduce you to him. Would you like that?"

"Sure." What a cool cousin.

We drove back to the cottage on the narrow road, the steep, green Alborz Mountains to our right, the calm waters of the Caspian Sea to our left.

Our vacation in Shomal was the perfect retreat. For a short time, I forgot about Tehran and how everything there seemed to be changing. But when it was time to leave, it all came back to me in a rush, and I wondered what awaited us upon our return.

It was a letter.

Maman opened it. It was from her boss at the French multinational oil company where she had been working for the last three years. After reading it, she wearily brought her arms down and said, "Well, they've done it. They've closed the office and gone back to France." She leaned her head against Baba's shoulder.

Baba rubbed her back and tried to console her. "You'll find another job. Don't worry."

Maman sighed and said, "I wonder what Christine is going to do." Christine was Maman's French friend and my best friend Anahita's mother.

Christine and Maman spoke on the phone for nearly an hour.

Toward the end of their conversation Maman said, "Let me think about it. I'll call you back tonight." She hung up and said, "That was Christine."

"We know," Baba and I said.

Maman giggled and continued, "She just told me that Razi is no longer offering a French curriculum. All the French teachers left this summer."

"So I will only have Persian classes from now on?" I asked.

Maman nodded. She explained to us that Christine and several other French women were going to start teaching for the French Center for Distance Learning, or FCDL.

"They want me to join forces with them and start teaching a group of students," Maman said.

"How does the program work?" Baba asked.

"Apparently through the French Embassy. Christine has already been in discussions with the consul."

The embassy would provide annual curriculums, with all the lessons, exercises, and homework. Maman said this was done for expatriates, or French-speaking people living outside of France.

"But who would your students be?" I asked.

"The Razi students who want to continue their bilingual education and get a French diploma."

"All of them?" I said.

"Of course not. Christine said we would offer the FCDL program for first through fifth graders. It will be easier to teach the younger kids. After meeting with interested parents, we'll have a better idea of how many students each of us would have."

After a long pause Baba said, "Is this something you want to do?"

Maman smiled and said, "I do. I think it's a good opportunity. Besides, it'll show the Islamic Republic that the French never give up."

That evening, Maman called Christine and said, "I'm in."

The next day, Maman told me we were invited to Christine's house for lunch.

"Wear old clothes. You and Anahita can pick cherries in their garden!"

Anahita lived just five minutes from our apartment, in one of the few houses in our neighborhood. Most people in Tehran lived in apartment buildings, both large and small. Anahita's family lived in a home with a big backyard. Toward the rear of the yard, a hammock stretched between two huge weeping willow trees.

Cherry trees formed a fragrant border around the rectangular swimming pool. Near the house, lawn furniture was arranged on a tiled patio where a brick structure held a barbecue. Their house smelled of jam and cookies, and lace doilies decorated every piece of furniture. I loved going there to play with Anahita.

Christine greeted us with open arms. She had fine, short brown hair and always wore pants with long blouses. She had married and moved to Iran in the late 1950s. Anahita was born years later. Christine led me to the back, where Anahita was arranging buckets near the cherry trees. Anahita wore a red shirt and black overalls, and she had pulled her long brown hair into a ponytail. A wooden ladder had been set up near one of the trees. Before leaving us to our work, Christine said, "Enjoy this beautiful day, girls."

Anahita and I ate as many cherries as we picked.

"Can you do this?" Anahita asked. She popped a cherry into her mouth, and then pulled a knotted cherry stem out. After several failed attempts to make my tongue do the same trick, I gave up and said, "Nope. But I can wear cherry earrings. Look," I said, dangling the red fruit from my ears.

An hour later, Christine called us in for lunch. She had made us a typical three-course French lunch. For the first course, we had deviled eggs, *jambon,* and *saucisson* (French ham and sausage that we could only find on the underground black market because eating pork is forbidden in Islam), and a large *salade niçoise.*

For the second course, Christine brought a tray of cheeses with baguette slices. Maman gasped.

"Brie, Camembert, and a Roquefort," she said. "Christine, you must have spent a fortune on these cheeses."

"Not really. I have a friend who sells luxury goods. He gives me good deals."

"I've been starved for a piece of France lately!" Maman exclaimed. "This really is the ultimate luxury."

Then came the pièce de résistance: For dessert, Christine unveiled a *clafoutis,* a lovely custard baked with whole cherries. I looked at Maman when she said, "Christine! This is my favorite dessert." The expression on her face made my heart tighten for her. That a simple dessert could make her so happy told me how much she missed her home. I said, "Maman, I can help you make clafoutis any time you want." She smiled and took a big bite of the dessert, savoring the taste, and no doubt the memories brought with it.

Maman leaned back in her chair and said, "We are going to have to be very careful if we do this."

Do what? I thought. Eat cherries?

"We will," Christine said. "I am so glad you agreed to it. I can't stand having these zealots telling us what to do or not to do."

"Then again, after a meal like this I keep thinking, what are we still doing here?" Maman said. "We should just go back to France."

Christine laughed while Anahita and I stared at each other.

"I love Iran," Christine said.

"I don't love it so much anymore," Maman said. "But I do like the idea of defying this regime and starting an underground school."

Oh, the teaching thing. "What does 'underground' mean, Maman?" I asked.

"It means something you do in secret so nobody finds out. In our case, we don't want the Iranian government to find out."

"Sounds risky, doesn't it?" Christine said. She giggled like a schoolgirl.

"We definitely run the risk of getting into a lot of trouble if we're caught teaching a coed group of kids," Maman said. Oddly

enough, she didn't look concerned at all—more like a mischievous fire had lit her up from within.

"It's going to be wonderful," Christine said. Maman laughed and squeezed my shoulder.

Christine suggested we drive to the building where the Alliance Française, the French club, used to meet to see if they could hold these new classes there. We went to a historic quarter of Tehran, nearly 45 minutes from our neighborhood. Because of the distance, Maman and I had never attended any of the events at the Alliance.

It was housed in a two-story, ivy-covered stone building surrounded by a large garden with pomegranate and walnut trees. A groundskeeper who lived on the estate gave us free rein to look around. Many of the rooms on the first level held random desks and chairs. On the second floor we discovered a dusty library filled with leather-bound classics, including Alexandre Dumas, Molière, and Victor Hugo.

We also found a long rectangular room with cheerful yellow walls covered in large posters of French film stars like Brigitte Bardot, Alain Delon, Catherine Deneuve, and Jean-Paul Belmondo.

As soon as Christine saw this room, she clapped and said, "This is it! This space will be great for a classroom. What do you think?"

"It's perfect," Maman said.

Christine turned her attention to Anahita and me, busy trying to imitate Brigitte Bardot's famous pout, and she said, "The Islamic Republic says it is not possible for the French to teach in this country? Well, *impossible n'est pas français!* Nothing is impossible, girls! Nothing."

I hoped she was right.

REBELLION
1980–1981

Din o donya do zede yekdigarand.
—Persian proverb

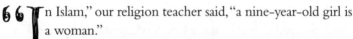

Religion and the world are against each other.

"In Islam," our religion teacher said, "a nine-year-old girl is a woman."

"Why does Islam say this?" I asked, feeling very much like a nine-year-old girl, and not at all like a woman.

I tugged at the collar of my navy robe, our new mandatory school uniform, with its stiff fabric scratching my neck. Our school had said wearing a scarf was optional, though highly encouraged. Maman had not bought me one.

"Because girls can start menstruating at that age," the teacher said. "That is why girls have to cover themselves in front of men because they are tempting to them."

"Gross," I whispered.

I hate the way Religion class forced these beliefs down our throats. During recess, I complained incessantly to Anahita about that class, and especially about the teacher.

Bianca heard me talking to Anahita and joined our conversation.

She had disappeared from school last year, after her father's execution. When she returned, she said she never wanted to talk about what had happened. Even though we wanted to ask her questions, we didn't.

She said, "You should pretend to be Christian."

"Why?" I asked.

"To skip out of Religion class." She shrugged. "Like me."

Bianca was Christian-Armenian, so she didn't have to take Religion class.

"Bianca, you're allowed to skip it because you're not a Muslim," Anahita said.

"They can't force you to study another religion," Bianca said.

"Yes, they can," Anahita said.

"Wait, Bianca, do you think the teacher will believe me if I say I'm Christian?" I asked.

"She might," Bianca said. "She doesn't seem very bright."

"Bianca, that's a brilliant idea." I thought for just a moment and said, "I'll do it."

Bianca jumped down from the bench where she'd been perched and hugged me tightly against her chest.

"You're both crazy," Anahita said.

"Why? This is great. I won't have to go to this ridiculous class anymore."

"Fine. But I still think you're crazy," Anahita said.

At home, I thought about what Anahita had said. Perhaps she was right. But I didn't like how closed-minded most of our new teachers were. Baba's family was Muslim, yet they never said or did anything that sounded against my beliefs. They had welcomed Maman, a French woman, with open arms and celebrated her holidays to make her feel at home.

~

I'll never forget our first Christmas in Iran, when I was five years old. All the weather signs had indicated my favorite time of the year

60

was near. The air was cold, and snow covered the Alborz Mountains north of the city. But I had one burning question on my mind: Would Santa Claus come to Iran? Had anyone informed him that I now lived on a different continent?

In Pittsburgh, I knew Christmas was coming because of all the wreaths and lights around the city, and the life-size sleigh packed with presents in our neighbor's front yard. But here, aside from the cold, nothing suggested the holidays. I didn't hear "Frosty the Snowman" or "Jingle Bells," and no houses or stores displayed Christmas decorations. All I could see when looking out our living room window were orange taxicabs, street vendors selling roasted beets, and lots of people strolling along, just as they usually did.

None of this looked like Christmas. Somehow, I had to get word to the North Pole. I picked up a pen and a sheet of my Snoopy stationery and ran around the apartment looking for Baba. I found him napping on our new blue couch in the living room, with a book spread across his chest and the portable radio glued to his left ear. Surely, this letter to Santa was an urgent matter, so I shook him awake.

I dictated this letter to Baba:

Dear Santa,

My name is Nioucha. I used to live in Pittsburgh. My Baba moved us here so we could be near his family. I want to tell you that workers are renovating the kitchen in our new home. With all the mess, we can't celebrate Christmas here, so Aunt Minoo will host our party.

Will Rudolph know the way?

Can I have these presents please?

1. A yellow-and-blue canary, because I had to give Titi to my best friend Linda in Pittsburgh. Maman said I couldn't bring him with me on the plane to Iran.

2. *An Easy-Bake Oven. It was too big to put in a suitcase so I gave that to Linda too.*

3. *A new Barbie. My cousin Omid threw mine in their swimming pool. I can't get her out because she is under ice. She must be very cold.*

4. *Barbie clothes*

I have been good this year, and I hope you can come to Tehran. Omid does not deserve any presents. He is mean.

I'm sorry we don't have a chimney.

> *I love you Santa,*
> *Nioucha*

Baba folded the letter, put it in an envelope, and addressed it to Santa at the North Pole.

Just a few days before Christmas, Baba dropped me off at my grandparents' house so we could bake cookies for Santa.

When I walked in, Maman Bozorg clasped me to her chest and kissed the top of my head. She stood only slightly taller than me and wore a silk headscarf that had slid off her head. She had small brown eyes and a smile that lit up her whole face.

"I have a present for you," she said.

She handed me a child-size apron with white and dark blue paisleys set against a turquoise background.

"I made it especially for you," Maman Bozorg said. She spun me around to tie the bow behind me.

That's when I noticed the pictures of me on the wall, directly above the dining room sideboard. There were three of them, one for each year I had spent at the preschool I attended in Pittsburgh. In the first one, all the three-year-olds are seated in the wagons of a toy train set against a toy house. My short mop of brown hair

covers my forehead and most of my green eyes. The next two are variations on the first, except by the time we were five we could no longer fit in the wagons, so a number of us, including me, are sitting on the roof of the playhouse.

Noticing my stare, Maman Bozorg said, "You might have been living far away from me for the first years of your life, but you were always in my heart, my precious grandchild. Now, let's bake!"

"Where's Agha Jan?" I asked. I hadn't seen my grandfather since I'd come in.

"He's taking a nap. He hasn't been feeling well. We'll get him up before dinner."

She helped me climb up on one of the two kitchen stools, and I watched her skillful, delicate hand as she mixed the egg yolks, sugar, and walnuts with a wooden spoon. At first I was disappointed not to see any cookie cutters in the shape of a Christmas tree, reindeer, or Santa. After all, those were the ones that Maman used to bake sugar cookies with. But after a few minutes, I became completely absorbed watching Maman Bozorg.

Using her fingers, she scooped up the batter, formed perfectly shaped balls and lined them up on a cookie sheet. After she removed them from the oven, she let me sprinkle them with ground pistachios. The smell of those cookies was so intoxicating that I didn't notice that they looked nothing like Christmas trees or Santa. That night I was supposed to sleep at my grandparents' house. But as soon as dinner was over, I felt homesick and longed to go back to Maman and Baba. I was too embarrassed to tell anyone. So I hid under the dining room table, crying softly for my parents.

Maman Bozorg was cleaning in the kitchen, but Agha Jan saw me from where he sat on the couch. He continued to read the newspaper. After a few minutes, he reached for his cane and stood up, grunting with pain. I had heard that he had diabetes, which made him have lots of health problems.

Agha Jan walked to the dining table and propped his cane against a chair. He squatted down and moved his body as near to me as he could. I wiped at my tears, hoping he hadn't noticed me crying.

"Do you miss your mother?"

I nodded. And the tears came down even harder.

"Come here, precious," he said.

He opened his arms to me, and I moved next to his soft body as he awkwardly stayed on the floor with me.

"There, there," he whispered. "I know exactly how you feel."

"You do?"

"Sure. When I was a boy, my parents often sent me to stay with my grandparents and I used to miss my home terribly at first."

"So what did you do?"

"I just felt homesick the first night. Then I got used to it."

"But why did your parents send you away?"

"We were a big family, and my grandparents loved having me around so they could spoil me."

Agha Jan cupped my face in his large hands. He looked so much like my Baba, with the same kind of face you just wanted to kiss. I threw my arms around Agha Jan's neck and kissed his cheek. He laughed.

"If you miss your parents, I can call and ask them to pick you up. I don't want you to feel sad."

I thought about it for a second, but I didn't feel homesick anymore. I hugged Agha Jan and said, "No, I want to stay with you."

"That's good because I need your help getting out from under this table."

The next morning, Maman picked me up in a taxi. She had vowed never to drive in Iran because the traffic terrified her. As soon as we left my grandparents' house, Maman told me, "Minoo said she has a surprise for us!"

When we knocked on the door, Aunt Minoo opened it and then clapped her hands in excitement. She said, "I really hope you like it!"

"Like what?" I said.

"Come in, come in," Aunt Minoo said, pulling us both inside.

Maman let out a gasp of surprise as we stepped into the living room. She said, "It's the biggest Christmas tree I've ever seen."

I followed Maman's eyes. Near the fireplace stood the most amazing pine tree I'd ever seen inside a house. Our Christmas tree in Pittsburgh was made of plastic and wasn't much taller than I was. But this one was so huge and perfect that I jumped up and down singing, *Jingle bells, jingle bells, jingle all the way.*

Aunt Minoo laughed and said, "I want you to feel at home."

"It's beautiful," Maman said. "Where did you get a real tree?"

"I bought it in the Armenian neighborhood," Aunt Minoo said. "They celebrate Christmas."

"I love how fragrant it is," Maman said as she stepped closer and inhaled the pine scent in long, deep breaths. "Thank you, Minoo. This is absolutely lovely."

After hugging each other, Aunt Minoo asked, "Did you bring any of the ornaments you had with you?"

"No," Maman said. "I gave them all away."

"I can fix that," Aunt Minoo said. She pulled out a bag from behind the tree. In it were rolls and rolls of gold and red ribbon. "We can make large bows out of these and use them as ornaments."

"Wonderful," Maman said. "Nioucha, do you want to help us?"

"Yes," I said.

The three of us sat on the living room floor making bows for the Christmas tree. After we were done arranging them on the branches, Aunt Minoo took six chairs from the dining room table and circled them around the tree. She stepped onto the first chair and then walked from chair to chair, winding a red velvet ribbon from the top to the bottom and back up to the top again as she made her way around.

"Minoo," Maman said, "it's gorgeous. Thank you so much."

"You're welcome," Aunt Minoo said, beaming at Maman and me.

Finally, Christmas Eve arrived. I would soon find out whether Santa had received the letter. At Aunt Minoo's house, my cousins Omid and Sara had been tasked to keep a watchful eye on me in the TV room. It was their job to make sure I didn't sneak a peek at what went on in the living room, where Santa Claus was supposed to deliver the gifts.

I wore the new dress Maman bought from the boutique that sold French children's clothes. It was red velour with white lace around the collar, sleeves, and hem. Sara braided my long hair with a red ribbon. When she finished, she sat back and said, "You look so French with that dress and your hair like that."

Omid snapped, "That's because her mom is." He sat at the end of the couch and sulked with his arms crossed firmly on his round belly.

Sara shot him a dirty look and said, "Be quiet, Omid."

"*You* be quiet," Omid said.

I was getting used to their bickering and took advantage of their distraction to slip off the couch and get near the glass door that led to the patio. I slid behind the thick satin curtains hoping to get a glimpse of Santa and his sleigh. I glanced around the garden and into the sky, which looked like a black sheet punctured with bright white holes. That was one of the most striking things about Tehran: the sheer number of stars in the sky. Still, no signs of Christmas.

Omid joined me and said, "What are you doing?"

"I'm looking for Santa," I said.

"Maybe you'll see him better if you stand outside," Omid said. He opened the patio door and pushed me outside, slamming the door behind me and leaving me alone in the cold, dark night. Stunned, I turned around and tried to open the door, but Omid had locked it. He stood watching me, grinning and sticking his tongue out. Sara shoved him aside, sending a volley of curses at him, and opened the door for me. She pulled me in her arms and said, "I'm sorry, Nioucha. Are you all right?"

Then turning to Omid she added, "You are such a jerk!"

"I'm okay," I said, still surprised by what had just happened.

"Leave me alone," Omid said. He plopped back on the couch.

"Ignore him, Nioucha," Sara said. "He's always like this."

Omid looked up at his sister and I was almost sure he seemed remorseful.

Suddenly Aunt Minoo entered the library and announced, "Santa Claus just dropped off your presents."

"Just now?" I said. "But I didn't see him!"

"That's because he's not …" Omid started. Aunt Minoo gave him a sharp look and said, "That's because he came in through the back door."

She clapped her hands together, bouncing with joy. We ran into the living room, where the rest of the family greeted us with happy faces.

"Santa got my letter!" I said. "Santa got my letter, Baba!"

I threw myself in Baba's arms, ecstatic that Rudolph had found his way to Aunt Minoo's house. Baba laughed and directed me to the tree. As he busied himself with taking pictures, I noticed the plate of cookies I'd left for Santa was now empty.

"Maman Bozorg, look, Santa ate the cookies we made!" I said. She sat in an armchair near the tree, her hands folded in her lap. I ran into Maman Bozorg's arms and buried my face in her chest. She chuckled, and when she did, her whole soft, round body moved up and down.

"Maybe *I* ate all the cookies," Agha Jan said. He wore a three-piece brown suit and held his wooden cane with the silver handle in front of him.

"Agha Jan!" I said.

"Aga Jan is just joking," Maman said.

I noticed him covering his mouth with his hand and smiling under it. He motioned for me to come over. I climbed onto his lap. Agha Jan whispered in my ear, "I love your mother's pronunciation."

"So you don't mind that she can't say your name right? To her you're 'Aga,' not 'Agha.'"

"Oh, quite the contrary. I hope she never learns how to pronounce the *gh* sound properly. Her accent is so charming."

"Baba loves it when she speaks Persian too," I said.

"Look at all the gifts Santa brought," Maman said. Agha Jan and I looked at each other and nodded knowingly about Maman's lovely accent. The curlers she'd put in her hair before the party gave her hair a glamorous bounce, and the gray eye shadow made her blue eyes stand out even more.

A pile of presents spilled out from around the giant Christmas tree.

"Did Santa bring something for everybody?" I asked.

I worried whether Santa had listened to what I'd said in the letter and had not brought Omid anything. Seeing everyone so happy made me feel bad about wishing something so mean.

"Yes, he brought presents for you and your cousins," Maman said. "Go on, open them, chérie."

I slipped from Agha Jan's lap and sat among the presents. Sara started distributing the gifts. Soon, we were lost in a sea of toys and wrapping paper.

"This is our first Christmas," Sara said.

"Don't you love it?"

"Oh, I do."

"Well, this is wonderful," Agha Jan said. "I think from now on, we should adopt Christmas as a family celebration. This will help my daughter-in-law feel more at home. What do you think?" he addressed Maman Bozorg, who smiled and said, "If it's making our family so happy, why not?"

~

My grandparents, who were Muslim, had opened their hearts and minds to my mother's traditions. They were a true example of what their faith was really about. This was very different from the closed-minded things we were being taught at school. Maybe Bianca was

right. I wasn't sure how Agha Jan and Maman Bozorg would feel if I lied about not being a Muslim, but my mind was made up.

The following morning, I told the Religion teacher that I should be exempt from her class because I wasn't a Muslim, but a Christian. She knew Maman was French, so my lie seemed believable to her. It never occurred to her that Muslim children inherit their father's religion. Because Baba was a Muslim-Iranian, I was too. She immediately excused me from her class. Perhaps she was glad to see me go, because I kept questioning what she said and staring at her with frustration and anger.

That was how it all began. Throughout the week, I got to leave the Religion class along with Bianca and the other Armenian girls. We played board games in the library and volleyball in the playground. It was such a relief not to have to listen to that teacher.

At least I thought it was a relief, until the unexpected happened.

One morning two weeks before the end-of-year finals, I had run up and down the long school hallway, slamming the classroom doors shut. Now I can't figure out why I did it, but at the time I remember the thrill I felt from the sound of the slamming doors. All the doors had a large window at the top. One of the glass panes broke and shattered in a loud crash. A classmate who stood at the end of the hallway turned around and saw what happened.

"Nioucha, look what you did," she said.

"I didn't do it," I said. "You did!"

She called me a liar, and I called her something worse.

"I'm going to tell what you did!" she said, and marched toward the principal's office.

I followed her, hoping she was bluffing. On the way, I said, "All right, all right, I know I broke the glass. You don't need to go tell on me!"

But she kept walking, determinedly staring ahead. Before I could coax her further, she walked into the principal's office and told her I had broken the glass pane. She also said I had lied to the Religion teacher by telling her I was Christian when I was really Muslim.

An hour later, I was called out of geography class to go to the principal's office. Maman was already there, her face flushed. She waved me to her and put her arm around the small of my back. Her long blond hair was pulled back in a ponytail, something she only did when applying makeup. She wore a long beige robe over white pants and a brown T-shirt, and her white nylon scarf hung loosely around her neck.

The principal was mad, telling Maman my behavior was "just outrageous and inexcusable." I figured she had completely forgotten about the broken glass, in light of the "inexcusable" denial of my religion.

The Religion teacher, who sat next to Maman, told her while pointing at me, "Your daughter is going straight to hell for lying about her religion. You should be ashamed of yourself for raising such a child."

Maman refused to look at the teacher. The principal dismissed her.

As soon as the Religion teacher left, the principal told Maman, more calmly, that if it weren't for the fact that she knew our family well, she would be forced to expel me from school to show her support of the Islamic regime. Then she asked me to wait outside.

Minutes later, Maman came out, grabbed my hand, and told me I was skipping the rest of my classes and going home with her. We didn't speak a word to each other in the taxi. As soon as we were home, she started yelling at me.

"This is the worst thing you've ever done, Nioucha! Have you lost your mind to lie about such things? Don't you realize you could get our family in trouble with this new regime by not taking the Religion class? Don't you know our family has been under surveillance since your great-uncle fled Iran?"

I stood mute. Maman stared at me with her hand on her hip. But Great-Uncle lived in Switzerland now, so why were they watching us?

Maman must have read my mind because she said, "They don't

know he's escaped to Geneva, so they've tapped our phone lines to find out where he is."

"He left two years ago. Why are they still checking on us?" I asked.

"I have no idea," Maman said. Then, "Well, what were you thinking?"

After a long silence, I said, "I … I hated that class so much. The teacher said crazy things. I'm … I'm sorry."

"Nioucha, studying religion is mandatory for all Muslim children. Even if you don't like your teacher or your class, dodging it is a direct offense to everything the Islamic Republic stands for. Don't you understand that by now?"

"But Bianca told me I could …"

"I don't want to hear it. Go to your room."

She fumed in the kitchen for hours banging cabinets and slamming pots before Baba came home. I was mortified. I hid in my room all afternoon, barely breathing, afraid of attracting more attention to myself. I never thought that what I'd done could harm my family.

When Baba came, they whispered in the kitchen for what seemed like an eternity. I was certain they could hear my heartbeat through my door, the hallway, and the TV room. Then Baba laughed. I heard Maman's angry voice. They spoke in French with each other, only now that her Persian was so good, Maman interspersed her French with Persian phrases. I caught snippets from Maman—"good kid … trouble … bad grades … what happened?" Then from Baba—"not that bad … don't get carried away … yes, it's serious, but the principal will talk to the teacher I'm sure and explain that kids do silly things." Then, after more whispering, Baba proudly said, "daughter of my heart."

After a long silence, Baba called me into the kitchen. I walked in, holding my head down, deeply ashamed. Baba rarely got angry with me—Maman was the disciplinarian—but when he did, it was frightening. A stern "Nioucha" from him made me shrink into myself for hours.

"Your mother told me what you did." He stopped abruptly. I looked up. He was trying not to laugh. Maman nudged him. He cleared his voice and said, "Nioucha, you're in a lot of trouble. Your principal is very upset and so is your mother."

"I'm so sorry."

"We know you are. Look, I had to study religion when I was a kid, too."

"I know. It's just that it's coming from THEM. It gets me so mad!"

"You don't have to tell me," Baba said. "I'm having a hard time keeping my opinions to myself lately too."

He sighed and added, "In ten days, you have to take the final exam with the rest of your class."

My heart sank. "But how can I take the exam? I haven't even opened the book all year."

"Don't worry. We'll get you a tutor."

"But, Baba, I don't want to."

"You have no choice." He cupped my face in his hand, smiled, and said, "That'll be punishment enough for you, having to take the exam in a class you've been avoiding all year. You should be able to get a passing grade."

I spent endless, excruciating hours with my tutor studying Quranic verses, their meanings, the names of the prophets, and what they did. I slogged through the 300-page Religious History textbook and worried myself to sleep every night.

On exam day, I felt sick with anxiety. When the teacher handed out the test, I glanced quickly at all the questions. I was relieved after seeing I knew the answers to many of them. I wrote and wrote and wrote until my fingers ached. And somehow, all my studying paid off and I managed to get a passing grade. But I promised myself I would never try to pull off a lie like that again.

WAR

1981

To kaz mehnate digaran bighami
Nashayad ke namat nahand adami
—Saadi, Persian poet

You who feel no pain at the suffering of others
It is not fitting you be called human

When I was 10, they changed our school altogether, making it an all-boys school. Anahita and I were no longer allowed to attend. We felt terribly sad and rejected. Instead, we had to go to a middle school called Jahane Koodak, "A Child's World." Compared to the grandeur of Razi, this facility for girls seemed really puny. It was just an L-shaped two-story building with classrooms and a small auditorium. The playground was a drab, rectangular stretch of cracked asphalt.

Painted windows prevented passersby from looking into our dark, crowded classroom, located in a semibasement. The place had fallen into such disrepair that even the doorknob kept falling off. We sat on wooden benches designed to accommodate two children, but three of us were forced to squeeze in. I shared a bench with Anahita and another girl we didn't know. In fact, we hardly knew anyone in the entire school.

And that year, aside from only being with girls, I had to wear

a headscarf. The year before we'd gotten uniforms—long robes for girls. This school required the robes and now headscarves too. Even the little first graders had to cover their heads. Not only did we have to wear them in school but also out in public.

Maman bought me a navy scarf to match my robe from the Islamic garb store in our neighborhood. When she came home, she handed it to me and said, "Here, try it on."

I took the large square piece of fabric, folded it into a triangle just like I had seen Maman Bozorg do dozens of times, and slipped it on my head. I tied a knot under my chin and tucked in the loose strands of hair.

"How do I look?" I said, turning to face Maman.

"Ridiculous. Absolutely ridiculous. This is outrageous! How can you be required to wear a scarf?"

"I don't mind so much," I said.

"You are only a child!" Maman said.

"But, it's not my fault …" I said.

"No, of course it's not your fault, chérie. Of course not. This whole situation is just infuriating." She took a deep breath and added, "I didn't mean to say you look ridiculous. You don't. In fact, wearing the scarf makes your green eyes stand out even more. I meant that asking kids to wear scarves is ridiculous. I'm just so mad!"

"I'm sorry," I said, not knowing how to respond to her anger.

"It's fine," she said. "I'll get started on dinner. Meanwhile, you can set the table please."

"Okay," I said, glad to have an opportunity to be helpful, hoping it could lift her spirits.

The next day, a young soldier came to our class to lecture us on bombs. I actually looked forward to it, because it meant we didn't have to sit through a math lesson. Before coming in, the soldier asked the teacher through the door if we were "decent."

She answered, "Yes, all the girls have their headscarves on. You may enter now." As she said this, she scanned us with her fierce eyes and pointed to several girls who had strands of hair showing. They quickly tucked them away under their scarves. Her own scarf came so far down her forehead that we could barely see her eyes.

The soldier walked in and without looking up bellowed, "We are at war with Iraq!" We all jumped in our seats. "Saddam Hussein, the Iraqi dictator, invaded Iran over a territorial dispute!"

The soldier stood with his head bowed and his hands clasped tightly behind his back.

After a long pause, he said, "I understand that some of you have fathers, brothers, or cousins fighting at the front."

At this, three girls looked down. The soldier remained silent, and they began sniffling. Then he solemnly bowed his head and said, "Allah appreciates their service and sacrifice for their country. May *he* bring them safely home to their families."

The entire classroom grew quiet, respectfully waiting for the girls to regain their composure. The teacher went to one of them and gently rubbed her back. The other two were in the arms of girls who sat near them.

My heart raced. I hated that this soldier had come here and made these poor girls cry. This one was from the Basij, a group of young men that had joined the war at the encouragement of Ayatollah Khomeini. They had also been given the job of monitoring the streets for any signs of protest against the new revolutionary values. We saw them everywhere around Tehran. They pointed guns and shouted insults at their elders just because they could. Pushy and rude, they acted the opposite of how we'd been taught to show respect to adults. The new government had taken homes away from the rich and given them to families of the Basij. And now one of them stood in my classroom. It took all my strength not to shout at him, "Get out!"

The soldier said, "I am here to teach you about the three types of sirens that blare when we come under attack from the enemy: red code, white code, and yellow code." He wrote all three colors on the blackboard. He pointed to the first one and said, "Red code is for regular bombs. It sounds like an ambulance."

We all nodded, having heard the red siren far too often.

"White code is to let the city know the enemy planes are gone and we are now safe to go about our business," he said. "It is a long, drawn-out beep."

The soldier took a deep breath and underlined yellow. "This is for chemical bombs." But he didn't say what it sounded like. I felt all the hairs on my arms stand on end. I'd recently seen footage of Hiroshima's survivors on Iranian television. Horrific images of missing limbs, burn scars, and crooked infant skulls tormented my imagination. Getting bombed was bad enough, but the thought of chemical bombs made me want to curl up into a ball.

The soldier proceeded to write the following instructions on the blackboard.

What to do if the Iraqis drop a chemical bomb:
  1. Stay inside.
  2. Stand under the shower.
  3. Cover your mouth and nose with a wet towel.

"Iraq recently threatened to attack us with chemical bombs," he said, circling the numbers and putting large arrows next to each. "In case this happens, and pray to Allah it never will, follow steps one to three."

Naturally, we had a lot of questions to ask him. Anahita and I weren't going to let him have an easy time with the lesson he had just given us, terrifying us to our core.

"What if there are eleven people living in my house and we only have one shower?" Anahita asked, digging her elbow in my side. I knew there weren't 11 people living at her house.

"Do the best you can to keep your head under running water," he said. "Use the kitchen sink as an alternative."

"What if we have no clean towels to use?" Anahita continued.

"Find an item of clothing to use instead."

"What happens if we are out on the street when a chemical bomb falls on Tehran?" I asked, now digging into Anahita's side.

He blinked in horror and said, "Do the best you can to run inside your house as quickly as possible."

"But, what if at the time of the attack, I'm nowhere near my house?" I continued.

He winced.

"Run inside any house and soak your head in water."

At this, one of the girls who'd been crying earlier dissolved into tears again and wailed, "I want my mom! I want my mom!"

The teacher thanked the soldier, who mumbled a prayer as he left, and she rushed over to comfort the hysterical girl. Our class remained in a state of chaos until the bell released us from school.

That night, just as I was telling Baba about the lesson given by the Basij man, the red siren went off. The piercing sound made my heart sink. As usual, Maman grabbed her big Dior purse. She used it to store all our valuables: jewelry, cash, passports, and birth certificates.

"What's the point of carrying all that stuff when we're getting bombed?" I had asked her.

"Because if our building is bombed and we survive, we will have all our legal documents and some money in hand."

Baba grabbed the keys and we went down the stairs to our landlord's guest apartment. The first two floors of our building were his home, but he also had a furnished basement apartment for guests. Since the start of the war, the residents from the six apartment units had been taking refuge together in that basement apartment almost every night, or whenever the red sirens went off. He said the basement was very sturdy. If we got bombed, we would be safe down there.

New neighbors, a couple and their son, had moved in at the

beginning of the year. He was a pilot and she was a housewife. The son, Cyrus, was my age. I'd overheard the landlord say to Baba one night, "I think the pilot's wife suffers from depression. Apparently, her husband has girlfriends in most of Europe's capitals."

But I didn't care about that because the pilot gave us chocolates. He'd say, "Children, I brought bonbons. They're from Germany." Each bonbon was the size of a Ping-Pong ball with a hazelnut in the center. I liked to let the soft round ball melt on my tongue, and then when I could feel the hazelnut on the roof of my mouth, I crunched it and mixed it with the delicious milky bonbon.

Chocolates had become a luxury in Iran. Maman had recently wanted to buy some, but when she'd seen the price, she whispered to me, "This chocolate bar costs as much as two weeks' worth of groceries." I had continued to stare at the chocolate bar, wanting it so badly but knowing we had to walk away from it.

Each night when we hid from the bombing, Maryam, the landlord's daughter, led Cyrus and me into one of the apartment's side rooms to read us books. She liked to act like our big sister even though at age 12 she was only two years older.

What I really wanted was for Cyrus to like me. The first night he'd come to the landlord's guest apartment, I had tried hard not to stare at him, worried he could see how cute I found him. His large black eyes shined like the sparkling marbles Anahita kept in a jar on her nightstand. He looked like a miniature version of a pilot, all neat and well ironed. I had straightened up, trying to smooth my frayed braid, and walked over to where he sat alone on the couch and said, "Hi, Cyrus."

"Hi," he said. He stared hard at the floor. I waited for him to say something, but he never looked up. A little hurt, I joined Maryam in the guest room.

"It must be my clothes," I thought. "He probably likes girls with perfect outfits and perfect hair." For the next few weeks, I came

downstairs sporting well-combed hair and wearing matching tops and bottoms. But after we said hello to each other, he'd stare at anything but me. How could I get his attention?

When I started running out of nice clothes, I asked Maman to take me shopping.

"What?" Maman cried. "You've never taken an interest in shopping before."

"Sure I have," I said.

"No, not really," she said. "Is this about a boy?"

"No, Maman! Leave me alone." I left the room, but I saw the big smile on her face.

Maman took me to Gandhi Street, where we bought new clothes, including a purple skirt with a big yellow sun at the bottom and sunrays spreading up and around the fabric. I loved it, but I realized only too late that I didn't have any tops to match it. Or shoes.

That night, I had stood for at least 40 minutes in front of my closet trying to figure out what to wear. I pulled out my red-and-white dress with the cherry appliqués at the bottom, but then remembered I had worn it a few nights before. Instead, I chose a simple navy skirt, a white T-shirt, and navy espadrilles. I thought, "Maybe he'll like this outfit." Just then, the siren blared and the three of us went downstairs.

Cyrus and his family arrived at the basement apartment shortly after we did. I waited for him to look at me, but he didn't. I waved from across the room to him, mouthing "hi," and he waved back barely lifting his head. My heart sank. Once again he didn't notice me or my outfit. I was getting tired of the effort. When Maryam invited us to join her in a side room so she could read us books, I reluctantly followed her in.

"Any special requests tonight?" Maryam asked.

"No," Cyrus said.

"Okay," Maryam said.

She looked through the books that sat in stacks on the floor. She picked one and leafed through the pages.

"I'll stand up so you can see me better as I read to you," Maryam said.

I was suddenly so mad I could hear the blood pounding in my ears. Why did I have a crush on Cyrus anyway? It dawned on me that he was pretty boring. And I had wasted all this time trying to get him to like me when I didn't really like him after all. He was cute, yes, but that was all.

"Look, Maryam," I blurted. "I'm in sixth grade. I'm not a baby. I can read my own books."

I stood up from the twin bed Cyrus and I sat on and started to leave the room.

"I know," Maryam said. "I just … I like to read out loud … it helps me forget we're about to get bombed."

"Oh," I said. "Okay, go ahead and read, then."

I sat back down on the bed. Cyrus hadn't moved or reacted to my outburst. It figured.

"Do you kids have a candle in there?" someone yelled from the living room. "The power will go out soon."

Boom! The entire building shook.

"Kids, get out here right now," the same voice yelled. The three of us ran into the living room and sat next to our parents.

"They forgot to cut the power tonight," Baba said.

"I'll turn off the lights," the landlord said.

Even though we were in the basement, the living room and bedrooms had windows. *Boom!* Everything rattled.

"My god, that one was really close," the pilot said. We sat in the dark. The landlord had forgotten to light the candles. I sat sandwiched between Maman and Baba. They each had an arm around me. *Boom!* I felt the vibration in my chest and I jumped.

"Don't be scared, Nioucha," Baba said. But I heard the fear in his voice.

In the darkness, I saw Maryam's outline shake with silent sobs. She had her head in her mother's lap. *Boom! Boom! Boom! Boom!*

"They sure are hitting our neighborhood tonight," the landlord whispered.

The next one will fall on us, I kept thinking. The next one will kill us all.

Dozens of bombs fell all around us, one after the other. The sound was deafening and terrifying. A giggle built in my stomach and erupted from my mouth.

What's so funny? You're about to die! my mind screamed to myself.

"Calm down, chérie," Maman said, gripping my shoulder.

The tremors from the bombs made a glass fall from the coffee table. The glass shattered, but nobody moved to clean it up. To resist panicking, I thought about another time when I had heard glass shatter. It happened on one of the last days I saw my beloved Agha Jan.

~

Baba and I had come to my grandparents' house to check on Agha Jan because Maman Bozorg was making a two-day pilgrimage trip to Mashhad. After ringing the doorbell but getting no response, Baba had turned the key to let us in.

"Agha Jan?" Baba called out.

No answer.

"Agha Jan?"

We heard glass breaking. Baba ran toward the noise. It came from the small alcove to the side of the kitchen. Agha Jan liked to take naps on a small cot in there because it was cozy. I stood near the entrance, too frightened to go closer, but I could hear Baba saying over and over, "Agha Jan, are you all right? What's wrong? Are you okay? What happened?"

Finally, Baba came out of the alcove, supporting Agha Jan and walking very slowly toward me. Agha Jan looked ashen. His white

shirt collar was covered in blood, and he held wads of tissue in his hand.

"I'm taking you to the clinic right now," Baba said.

"Yes," Agha Jan said in a whisper.

I couldn't get any words out. I had never seen my grandfather in anything other than a three-piece suit. I ached to see him looking so haggard and old.

The clinic was mere steps away from their home. Still, it took an eternity to get there because Agha Jan had such difficulty moving his legs.

As soon as we walked in, a nurse came to us and asked, "What happened?"

"My father cut his ear on a broken piece of glass," Baba said.

"How did he do that?" she said.

"His cane slipped out of his hands when he was trying to get up from his nap and it broke the window near his bed. A shard of glass must have fallen by his head."

"I'm terribly sorry. Let's move your father to the examining room so a doctor can have a look at him."

Baba turned to me and said, "Wait right here for me."

Baba helped the nurse move Agha Jan somewhere behind a curtain, and I waited in the reception area. Not long after, Agha Jan came out with a bandage on his ear. He seemed steadier on his feet. Agha Jan winked at me and motioned for me to come closer.

"How do you like my new ear?"

I walked up to him, relieved to see his joking self again, and I put my hand under his arm.

"It looks like a snowball."

He chuckled. Agha Jan's ear had been patched up, but I could see that he was still in pain.

~

I was jerked from that memory as more bombs exploded. It was impossible to focus on anything except the horror of the moment.

I didn't know what would happen to us. Even if we survived this bombing, could we ever get over this terrible fear?

The crashes and explosions gradually sounded farther away. I tried to gauge which neighborhoods were being hit, but that made me think of Maman Bozorg, and Aunt Minoo and her family, and Anahita. I shut my eyes tight and began to chant a prayer from the Quran we'd learned at school called *Ayatol Korsi* (the Throne Verse). Our teacher had said, "After you recite the prayer, blow a puff of air in a circular motion to protect whomever you think needs protection."

Allahu la ilaha illa huwa Al-Haiyul-Qaiyum … wa hu wal 'Aliyul-Adheem.

Please, God, protect my family, Maman Bozorg, Aunt Minoo and her family, Anahita, and everybody.

Foooooof.

"They're leaving," Baba said.

I opened my eyes. Minutes later, the white siren roared. The landlord turned the lights back on. Maryam wiped her face. Cyrus looked pale. Still silently reciting Ayatol Korsi, I remained glued to Maman and Baba.

"This one was pretty serious," Baba said aloud, echoing what I already felt.

"The biggest attack so far," the pilot said.

The white siren stopped.

"Well, we should probably get going so we can call family and friends and make sure everybody is all right," Baba said.

Everyone stood up and began to say their goodbyes. Maryam came up to me, still wiping at her eyes. I gave her a hug and whispered, "Sorry. You can keep reading us books if you want to."

"Thanks," she said.

Cyrus came behind her and waved, staring at the floor. I didn't bother waving back. He wasn't even looking at me, so how could he see what I did or didn't do?

"Kids, take some more bonbons," the pilot said. "Tonight was tough on all of us."

EXPECTATIONS

1982

Behesht zire paye madaran ast.
—Persian proverb

Heaven is under the feet of mothers.

I wandered into the kitchen and found Maman standing near the dishwasher, gripping her swollen belly with one hand and the kitchen counter with the other, her face contorted in pain. I froze and stared at her.

"It's time," she said. "Go call Baba and tell him to come home right away."

I ran into the TV room, grabbed the receiver, and dialed Baba's office at the radio station.

"Baba, come home. Maman has gone into labor. She looks like she's dying!"

After hearing Baba say he was on his way, I ran back into the kitchen. Maman looked relaxed now. The last few months of her pregnancy, she'd been wearing colorful Indian dresses popular in Iran since the war had begun. She had several of them, all with delicate floral patterns and gold thread trims. On this special day, she wore the fuchsia one. My favorite.

"Baba will be here soon."

"Good. Now, get ready so we can all go to the hospital together."

I changed into a pair of jeans and a clean T-shirt, put on my Nikes, robe, and scarf, and paced my bedroom, too scared to go into Maman's room and find her in pain again. I strained my ears for sounds of heavy breathing. A few minutes later, I walked into the TV room. Maman sat calmly on the couch, also wearing her robe and scarf, with a small suitcase at her feet.

"Are you ready?"

"Yes, Maman. Are you going to be okay?"

"Of course. It's going to hurt, but that's expected. Soon, you'll have a little brother or sister. Aren't you excited?"

I had been overjoyed when Maman announced her pregnancy. I was eleven years old, and I'd been begging her for a brother or sister ever since I was five.

"I don't know," I said. "You looked like you were going to die!"

She laughed. "What are you talking about? I'm not going to die. I'm going to give birth. Besides, I have a wonderful doctor. You have nothing to worry about."

But I was worried.

"Remember what we talked about? If it's a boy, we'll name him Nima. If it's a girl, Natalie."

"What do you think it'll be?"

She rubbed her belly and said, "It's not important, so long as the baby is healthy."

Baba stormed in, shouting, "I'm here, I'm here." He was completely out of breath. "Is everything okay? Michelle, are you okay?" He yelled as if Maman had gone deaf.

"Yes, we're fine." She patted me on the knee.

"Oh, thank goodness I made it home so fast. I found a taxi right away and there was no traffic. I worried it would take me longer to get here." He looked like he might burst into tears from relief. He wiped his glasses with his handkerchief. "Well, what are we waiting for? Let's go!" He helped Maman off the couch and grabbed her suitcase with his other hand. He ushered her out and into our white Chevrolet.

Baba usually took public transportation to work, but for this trip to the hospital, he was determined to be in the driver's seat. The Chevrolet was so ancient it frequently broke down at the most inopportune places, causing Baba to have serious meltdowns while Maman and I pretended not to hear his cascade of curses at the car. I could only hope it worked perfectly on this important mission.

I jumped in the backseat, Baba took the wheel, and we peeled away. Maybe Baba hadn't seen much traffic when he came home, but now every car and bus in the city seemed to have congregated on the streets where we wanted to go. Baba tried to maneuver our way through the sea of taillights, but progress was slow. Maman spoke with him about ordinary things. I was stupefied with anxiety. I asked myself, How long will it take us to get to the hospital? What if she goes into labor right here in the car?

I kept peeking at Maman to see if she looked all right. I fretted silently: Why is there always so much traffic in this city? It felt unusually hot for a May afternoon. We rolled all the windows down, letting in the noxious exhaust fumes. Suddenly, Maman stopped mid-sentence and shut her eyes tightly. She squeezed the purse she held in her lap so hard that her knuckles turned white. Maman had told me about these pains she called contractions. They sounded horrible.

"It's okay, just take deep breaths, my love," Baba said. "We'll be at the hospital in no time."

I wondered how he managed to remain calm. He spoke in a soothing voice and rubbed Maman's thigh. The contraction passed after what seemed like an eternity. Maman turned her head and smiled at both of us. I exhaled loudly.

We reached a checkpoint. We had entered an area of Tehran closed off during peak hours to control the flow of traffic.

Only government officials, residents, and the military could pass through freely at any time.

A young officer leaned into the window and said, "Let me see your official papers."

"Young man, my wife is in labor," Baba said, handing him the documents. "We're on our way to the hospital. Let us through quickly."

The officer peered into the car and noticed Maman's condition. He returned the papers to Baba and waved us through. Within minutes, we reached the hospital, parked right in front, and took Maman to the labor unit. A nurse led her into a private room. When I tried to go in, she held me back and slammed the door.

That door slam made me jump. Even though we hadn't been bombed for a couple of months, loud bangs still startled me. Iran and Iraq continued to be at war, but they had come to an understanding not to bomb the capitals for a while. This meant that the new baby would be born without the fear that I still held all the time.

Baba called Maman Bozorg and Aunt Minoo using the pay phone down the hall.

I sat in the empty waiting room, facing Maman's closed door. Baba paced the hallway as I stared at the clock. It was 5:38 p.m. The nurse came out of Maman's room and closed the door, but not before I'd caught a glimpse of her. She was lying on her side, in a purple robe, clutching her belly. Her face was bright and shiny. She saw me and tried to smile. I got up to go in, but the nurse barred my way again.

Aunt Minoo and Maman Bozorg arrived. They both wore light brown robes and headscarves.

"How did you get here so quickly?" Baba asked.

"I don't even know how I made it, brother," Aunt Minoo said. She spoke in a flurry of excitement and energy. She hugged me.

"She drove too fast," Maman Bozorg said.

"You're right, Mother, but we arrived safely."

"Nioucha, my child, how are you doing?" Maman Bozorg asked. She kissed my forehead.

"I don't think Maman is okay. Her face looks terrible and she is in a lot of pain."

Maman Bozorg chuckled and said, "My child, I gave birth to six children. It's the most natural process in the world. Your mother will be fine."

Baba resumed pacing.

"I'm going in to be with Michelle," Maman Bozorg said.

I tried to follow her, but Aunt Minoo snatched my arm and said, "No child should see her mother in pain. You stay right here with me."

I reluctantly sat back down. Aunt Minoo joined me. After a few minutes, she paced the hallway alongside Baba. The clock read 6:14 p.m.

A man approached Baba and Aunt Minoo. I couldn't hear what they were saying but there were vigorous handshakes and head nods. It was the doctor. He entered Maman's room and stayed there for a while. It was 7:02 p.m.

When he came out, he smiled broadly at me and went through the double doors to the right. I stared at the doors until they stopped flapping. The doors read "Delivery Room." I hadn't noticed the sign before. At 7:16 p.m., the nurse wheeled Maman out to where we waited and then into the delivery room. On her way, Maman smiled and blew me a kiss.

Maman Bozorg came and sat beside me. She put her arm around my shoulder and pulled me in. Aunt Minoo stood in front of us, absently picking her lips.

"Where's Baba?"

Aunt Minoo said, "He went outside to smoke a cigarette."

We sat in silence. The nurse came by and informed us that everything was going well. I breathed a sigh of relief. Baba returned. He clasped his hands behind his back, shifting his weight from one foot to the other.

"Nioucha, are you hungry?" Baba asked. "Do you want me to get you something from the cafeteria?"

"No thanks. I can't eat right now."

"How about you, Mother? Minoo? Can I get you anything?"

Aunt Minoo shook her head no.

"I'll have a tea, please," Maman Bozorg said.

Baba left before she'd finished her sentence.

"It's better to keep men occupied in these situations," Maman Bozorg said. "Otherwise, they go crazy."

It was 8:11 p.m. Baba came back and handed a plastic-foam cup to Maman Bozorg. She sipped her tea.

The nurse held the double doors open and announced, "It's a boy! Congratulations!" The four of us jumped and screamed with joy.

"How's my wife?"

"She's doing great. It was an easy birth. You'll be able to see her soon." She disappeared behind the double doors.

We hugged, kissed, and squeezed each other. It was 8:27 p.m. My dream had come true. Goose bumps ran along my body.

The nurse came out, pushing a small trolley. In it, there lay a green bundle.

"Do you want to see him?" she asked.

She pulled aside a corner of the green sheet. Baba, Maman Bozorg, and Aunt Minoo bent over the bundle. They made *ooh* and *aah* noises, cooing and gurgling to the baby. I couldn't see anything. The nurse took my hand and gave me her place. I saw him. He was red, wrinkled, and gross-looking. I stood back in horror. Was this really my brother?

The nurse noticed and said, "We haven't washed him yet. Come by the nursery later and have another look at him."

Another nurse pushed Maman out on a bed with wheels. Baba rushed over and showered her hand with fervent kisses. The nurse wheeled her into a private room. She looked exhausted but beautiful.

"Did you see him?" she asked all of us.

"He's perfect," everyone said, except for me. "Congratulations!"

Had they looked at the same baby I had? Gingerly, I approached Maman. I noticed a large black-and-blue mark on her arm.

"What happened?" I asked her, pointing to the bruise.

"It's nothing. They couldn't find my vein for the IV drip, so it bruised like this."

Maman Bozorg said, "We should let you get some rest. We'll come see you tomorrow morning."

Baba kissed Maman on the forehead and caressed her cheek. He whispered something and she beamed at him. He pulled out a box from his pocket and handed it to her. She opened it. Inside lay two gold bracelets she'd been coveting at the jewelry store in our neighborhood. She put them on and smiled.

Once we left her room, Aunt Minoo said, "Do you want to see your brother again?"

I did want to see him again, but I also worried he would still look weird. Aunt Minoo must have noticed my expression because she said, "The nurses will have cleaned him up by now."

"Definitely, then. Let's go!"

We made our way to the nursery and stood behind the glass separating us from the newborns. There were many small beds with tiny swaddled babies in them.

"How do we know which one it is?" I asked.

"Wait here." She knocked on the door of the nursery and said something to the nurse who had opened it. The nurse found the right bundle after reading the name tags at the bottom of each crib, lifted it, and held it near the glass where we stood. Her sharp, impatient movements made me scared she'd hurt the bundle.

"There he is," she said through the glass. "There's your little brother."

I stared at him. He was the most beautiful baby I had ever seen. He no longer had any wrinkles or gooey stuff on him. He opened his eyes and I noticed they were gray. For a second, he looked directly at me, and in that moment, I longed to hold him. His puckered lips were pomegranate red and his perfect little nose sat delightfully above them. He had dark brown hair only on the top of his head and nothing on the sides. I adored him. How could anything so small be so magical?

Aunt Minoo took me to her house for the night. Sara had gone to Shomal for a few days with my uncle. As I was about to enter Sara's bedroom, Omid emerged from his room, holding a jar of Nutella out to me.

"This is for you," he said.

"Is this a prank?" I asked.

"No!" Omid exclaimed. "I just know how much you like Nutella, that's all."

"So you're saying I'm fat?"

"What? No, you're beautiful."

"Okay, now I know this is a joke."

"Just take the Nutella."

"Wait a minute. Are you going to hold me upside down from the banister again if I take it?"

"No, I won't."

"Okay, this is just too weird. Forget it."

I tried to move past him, but Omid took a step toward me, extending his arm farther.

"I got this from the black market especially for you. It's to congratulate you on being a big sister."

When I continued to look at him suspiciously, he added, "Okay, I'll just set it on the floor and leave. Enjoy your Nutella."

He returned to his room and closed the door while I stood glued to my spot, staring at the jar at my feet, not understanding what had just happened. Who was this nice boy, and what had he done with my annoying cousin? I picked up the Nutella, walked into Sara's room, and curled up in her bed. What a strange day it had been.

I thought about the little baby boy across town as I drifted to sleep thinking, "Hi, Nima. Welcome to the world. I love you so much."

SPACES
1983

Manteghe poshte kalamatat ra bala
bebar na sedayat. Baran ast ke gol ha ra
parvaresh midahad na sa'eghe.
—Rumi, Persian poet

Raise your words, not voice. It is rain that grows flowers, not thunder.

I tried hard to tune out the words our eighth-grade Religion teacher fed us. She was beady-eyed and had a mustache above her mean-looking lips.

But frustration still got the better of me.

"Why did God test Abraham by telling him to sacrifice his son?" I asked her. "If God is God, then why does he need to test anybody?"

My teacher frowned, shook her head, lowered her eyes, and said, "Nioucha, you will burn in hell for not believing in God's commands."

"Yes, but can you explain to me why God needed to test Abraham? I just think it's a very cruel thing to ask of someone. I mean, killing your own son must be—"

"Stop! I don't want to hear another word from you!"

I shrugged. She may have been an adult, and I was only twelve, but still I knew she didn't have an answer. That's why she got so mad. A while later, I raised my hand to ask her another question.

Reluctantly, the teacher nodded and I asked, "Why do we have to protect men by covering our bodies? I mean, why did God make our bodies so tempting? Why don't men wear blinders so they're not led into temptation by our bodies?"

My teacher gave me a piercing look.

"Nioucha, for every strand of hair a man sees on your head, you will dangle from that hair in hell's fires for eternity."

I frowned because the image of hanging from one hair wasn't plausible. Wouldn't the hair break? I opened my mouth to protest but stopped because she looked furious.

"Nioucha, you shouldn't provoke these people," Anahita whispered.

"I'm just asking her a few questions," I whispered back. "She should be able to answer them without getting so mad. I mean, I have a right to ask questions about religion since she's the *religion* teacher."

"Just drop it," Anahita said. "You can't have a reasonable conversation with these fanatics about anything. Besides, do you want to get in trouble again like you did in fifth grade?"

"No, but …"

"Look, you don't have much choice but to sit there like the rest of us and pretend to listen."

Finally, the bell released us from school. Anahita and I made our way to her house.

Our mothers had successfully started the French school classes, but in the fall of 1982, when Nima was just three months old, Maman had realized she didn't want to commute to the Alliance Française. It was just too far away. So she started offering the classes in our home, and Christine had done the same. On Mondays, Tuesdays, and Wednesdays, Maman taught from three to six in the afternoon.

Ever since our mothers had been offering the French home-schooling, Christine had taken to coming over after lunch during

My Maman (left) and my Aunt Minoo and Uncle
Massoud during a visit to the United States in 1973.

This picture of my parents and me was taken in Pittsburgh, Pennsylvania, in 1976, two months before we moved to Iran.

Here I am (center, left) with my cousins Omid (back) and Sara (center, right) with our younger cousins on Christmas Day 1980 in Iran.

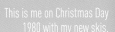

This is me on Christmas Day 1980 with my new skis.

Me, Maman, and Nima at Aunt Minoo's house, Iran, 1982.

Here I am wearing my headscarf. This picture was taken in 1987 while on a trip to the city of Mashhad in northwestern Iran.

This is the front of our apartment building in Tehran. We lived on the third floor. I would often look out this window at the view of the Alborz Mountains (shown below).

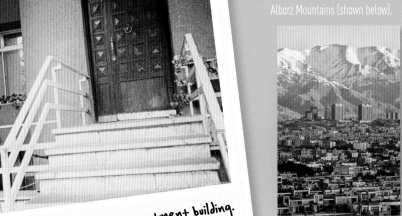

The front door of our apartment building.

This street in my neighborhood was part of my route to and from school each day.

This picture of Vanak Square in Tehran was taken during my 1998 visit. Vanak Square is a busy traffic and pedestrian hub in the city.

Baba buying barbari bread at a bakery in
Tehran during our 1998 visit.

My brother, Nima, and me at our parents' house in Pittsburgh, 1998.

Nima's nap so they could talk. Maman and Christine stood in the kitchen, drank black coffee, and spoke in hushed tones for fear of waking up Nima.

I, in turn, had been spending a lot of time at Anahita's house ever since Nima had been born. There, we could play music loudly and I didn't have to worry about bothering my little brother. Plus, Anahita had a gorgeous, large bedroom decorated in pale greens and yellows. Her canopy bed had a matching boudoir dresser, very grown-up compared to my furniture. Although I loved my bedroom, all in white and blue, with its very own balcony, I had outgrown the furniture soon after Baba had assembled everything. Even at six I didn't need the guardrails on my bed, or the big knobs on the dresser, desk, and the under-bed drawers. But the Scandinavian store where my parents had bought my set had long since closed, and I never asked them for a new one. Now, at 12, I definitely preferred Anahita's mature environment over my childlike one.

But every time I came to her house, I couldn't help being reminded of her eighth birthday party, even though it had been four years before. On that same day, I had found out my Agha Jan had died.

~

At school, all Anahita had talked about was her upcoming birthday party.

"You're coming, right?"

"Of course I'm coming, Anahita."

"Good. I really want you there."

"I can't wait to give you the present I got you."

"Can you give me a hint of what it is?"

"No way. It's a surprise."

"Not even a little hint?"

"You'll just have to wait until tomorrow afternoon."

"Okay."

All 20 of us from class came to the party, plus some of Anahita's cousins and extended family. There must have been 25 of us kids running around outside. Her birthday was in late September, but the weather was so nice that we were all still in our summer clothes.

On the tiled patio, one large table held the food and another all the birthday presents. The pool was covered in a dark green mesh to protect it from the falling leaves of the weeping willows. After we ate birthday cake, mine was the first present that Anahita opened. When she saw what it was, she gasped.

"Where did you get this?"

"What is it?" Christine asked.

"It's a Barbie airplane!" Anahita said.

"Maman got it from one of Aunt Minoo's friends," I said. "She travels to America once a year and brings back tons of toys and clothes to sell. Do you like it?"

"I love it so much. Thank you."

"You're welcome. You can't bring it to school with you since it's so big, but maybe we can play with it here, when I come over."

She gave me a hug and whispered, "This is the best present ever."

"Happy birthday, best friend."

She opened the rest of her presents, and then we all played and ran around the cherry trees. We paused now and then to eat more cake and triangles of watermelon, and drink tall glasses of *sharbat-e-sekanjebin*, a nectar made from mint leaves, vinegar, and sugar.

Then, as I chased after Anahita, something went crash behind us. We both turned around and saw everyone gathering around the sliding doors.

"What happened?" I heard a lot of kids ask.

Anahita and I pushed our way through the crowd, and that's when we saw that the sliding door had broken and shattered on the ground.

"What happened?" Anahita asked one of the kids there.

"Someone must have closed the sliding door and Bianca thought

it was still open. She ran through it."

"Oh no!" Anahita said. "Where is she?"

She pointed inside. We ran in and saw Bianca with Anahita's parents at her side. The front of her dress was covered in large drops of blood. Christine held a napkin on her chin, where she must have been cut. Bianca cried silently. At the sight of her, Anahita burst into loud tears and ran into Christine's arms.

"The blood is not stopping," Christine said. "We should take her to the hospital."

"I'll take her," Anahita's dad said. "You call her parents and let them know what happened."

As he led her away, Bianca turned around and said, "I'm sorry I ruined your party."

"You didn't," Anahita said.

"I'm going to round up all the kids," Christine said.

She went outside, where some of our classmates were still playing and asked them to come inside and wait for their parents to pick them up. She had us sit in the living and dining room to avoid any more accidents. We all sat there staring at the floor, not sure what to say or how to act after Bianca's terrible accident. I tried to console Anahita, but nothing seemed to cheer her up.

In the car ride home, I told Maman and Baba about Bianca falling through the glass door. I waited for one of them to say something, but when nobody spoke, I asked, "What's wrong?"

Baba glanced over at Maman and she put her hand on his forearm and turned in her seat to face me.

"Nioucha," Maman said. "Agha Jan ... He died this afternoon."

I screamed and cried at the same time, causing Baba to slam on the brakes even though we sat in traffic. Maman tried to calm me down, but I kept crying.

"No, no, no, no! Not Agha Jan."

"You know he was very sick with diabetes," Maman said.

"No, no, no!"

"I'm sorry, chérie," Maman said from the front seat. "He's not …
he's not hurting anymore."

"But … no!"

Baba reached around the seat and put a firm hand on my knee.
He didn't speak and kept his eyes glued to the road, but his touch
quieted me.

I couldn't absorb the news. I had just seen Agha Jan at the hospital two days before. Maman Bozorg had fought with the nurse who
wouldn't allow children in her section. When the nurse barred our
way, Maman Bozorg told her, "Listen, this might be the last time
she sees her grandfather."

Without another word, the nurse stepped aside. I hadn't understood what Maman Bozorg meant by "last time," until now.

Aunt Minoo stood by Agha Jan's bed trying to feed him soup, but
he wouldn't eat and was drifting in and out of consciousness. She
looked up when we walked in, and I was horrified to see that her
big green eyes were full of tears.

I kept staring at Agha Jan, hoping he would see me and motion
me over to him like he had done so many times before.

But he didn't.

The day after Agha Jan's death, my family held a memorial service
at Aunt Minoo's house. We arrived early to help with the prepara-
tions. They anticipated many people would come because Agha Jan
had a large family and lots of friends.

Maman and I went into the kitchen. The floor was covered
with large crates of apples, grapes, cherries, cucumbers, pomegran-
ates, and greengages, a small green type of sour plum common in
Iran. The kitchen table held four crystal bowls full of *ajeel,* a Persian trail mix of seeds, pistachios, and dried fruits. On the counters
were about two dozen boxes of pastries and cookies. Aunt Minoo
and Sara were busy placing fruit on huge silver trays.

When Maman looked all around the kitchen, she exclaimed, "I've
never seen so much food in my life!"

"Really?" Aunt Minoo said. "I'm worried there won't be enough. But there's nothing we can do about that now."

"Let us help you," Maman said.

She and I set to work. Aunt Minoo put me in charge of wiping the platters with a cloth and putting doilies on them before using them for the pastries.

Baba had explained that to follow religious customs, the men and women would mourn Agha Jan separately. Aunt Minoo had said that the men would be in the house and the women out in the garden, where there was a breeze.

We arranged many platters of food on the dining room table and brought the rest outside to put on the glass tables. In the covered stone portion of the garden, Aunt Minoo had placed dozens of metal chairs in a circle.

During the ceremony, which lasted several hours, helpers hired for the large gathering repeatedly came around with trays of hot tea.

I stayed outside with the women. All wore black and cried or moaned loudly. Maman Bozorg held me tight, rocking me in her lap and crying in my hair.

Anahita, who was there with her mother, waved me over but I didn't want to leave Maman Bozorg in this state, even though I didn't know how to comfort her. I waited a little to see if she would stop, but she never did.

Anahita waved again. I got up, but Maman Bozorg gripped my dress and pulled me back.

She whispered, "Agha Jan loved you so much. You were his little *Aroosak Farangi.*"

Some family members had been calling me that, their "European doll."

"And I loved him." I put my arms around her neck and kissed her cheek. "Do you remember the time he couldn't open the jar of mayonnaise?"

"Oh, yes."

"And you said, 'Give it to Nioucha. Maybe she can open it.' And I did! I opened it! And then Agha Jan laughed and said my skinny arms were as strong as a wrestler's."

From a young age, Agha Jan had shown such a passion for cooking that he had carefully followed the instructions his mother laid out to their cook until he had absorbed everything there was to know about Persian food. Maman Bozorg told me that as an 18-year-old bride, she didn't even know how to boil an egg. But over their years together, Agha Jan taught his wife everything he knew. With Agha Jan's encouragement, Maman Bozorg even started a small catering business.

"The secret to great cooking is top-quality ingredients," he told his bride. "Always buy the best you can find at the market and your food will be delicious."

Before long, Maman Bozorg had gained a reputation as an excellent chef.

On the day of the stubborn mayonnaise jar, Agha Jan had been keeping Maman Bozorg company while she made *cutlets,* one of her specialties. From my perch on the kitchen stool, I watched her knead the meat, onions, egg, cooked potatoes, turmeric, and other spices together until a smooth paste formed.

Agha Jan had stood nearby, occasionally looking over her shoulder, and saying, "I just want to make sure you're doing it right."

Then he'd laugh, knowing full well that she had long ago surpassed him in her cooking skills.

On the kitchen counter, Maman Bozorg had lined up the bowl containing the meat, another bowl of bread crumbs, and finally two trays. She had broken egg-size pieces off the mixture and formed perfectly shaped flat ovals in the palm of her left hand, then dipped the cutlets into the bread crumbs and placed them on the tray for baking.

"Maman Bozorg, how do you get the cutlets all the same size and shape?" I had asked.

She smiled and said, "Years of practice, my child."

I could watch Maman Bozorg for hours in her kitchen, and apparently so could Agha Jan. We admired her concentration and control over her work, combined with the agility of her hands. After the cutlets were golden brown on both sides, she let them cool. Then she placed before Agha Jan and me a plateful of them with fresh *taftoon,* a flatbread resembling pita bread, and a dollop of mayonnaise.

After eating a mouthful, Agha Jan had declared, "This is your best batch yet."

Maman Bozorg had giggled, suddenly looking much younger.

But now the burden of grief made my sweet grandmother look terribly old and broken.

"Your Agha Jan had a wonderful sense of humor," Maman Bozorg said. "He could turn anything into a joke." She squeezed me and said, "Now go play, my child."

I ran to Anahita.

"Are you okay?" she asked.

"Yes … no … I'm … sad and a little confused."

"My grandparents died before I was born."

"I know. That's too bad."

"Not really," she said. "I never knew them."

"Right."

I suddenly remembered her party.

"Hey, how's Bianca doing?"

"She got a few stitches on her chin. It wasn't too serious."

"Are you okay? About your party, I mean?"

"Yeah. I am now. Do you want to play soccer?"

"Sure. I'll go get the ball from the house."

"Wait, I thought we weren't allowed to go inside. All the men are there."

"Oh, I forgot."

"Try to sneak inside," Anahita said. "No one will notice."

"Hold on," I said.

I glanced around to see if I could find my cousin Sara anywhere, but I saw she was busy helping Aunt Minoo serve the guests with plates full of fruit and cakes. I reluctantly went up the few stairs leading to the house, opened the door, and peered inside. Omid stood right there.

"Omid, can you get me the ball from the coatroom, please?"

"Get it yourself." He turned his back and walked away.

I saw a crowd of men wearing black in the living room, mourning Agha Jan. Some cried while others spoke in hushed tones. I slipped inside the house, making myself very small, and went into the coatroom just to the right of the entrance. I found the ball under a pile of old seat cushions, stuck my head out to see if the coast was clear, and glanced around. My eyes landed on Baba.

He sat between his two younger brothers, hunched over and weeping into his hands. His entire body shook with convulsions. I could hear him over the sounds of everybody else. The ball slipped out of my hands and bounced into the living room.

Omid picked it up and handed it to me.

I kept staring at Baba, tormented by seeing him so sad. I wanted to go to him, sit in his lap, and kiss his tears. Because I wasn't moving, Omid grabbed me by the shoulders and led me outside. I didn't feel like playing anymore. I handed the ball to Anahita and returned to Maman Bozorg's arms, burying my face in her neck and trying hard to forget Baba's distorted face.

~

Although Anahita had celebrated three more birthdays since that sad day, I couldn't help associating each one with Agha Jan's death.

Now at 13, Anahita spent a lot of time on her looks. I wouldn't turn 13 for another six months and didn't feel as excited about makeup or getting dressed up as she did. I sat on the bed in her room and watched her. She concentrated on her dresser's round mirror and brushed her long hair. She took good care of it because she thought it was her best feature. I thought her hair was nice too, especially when it fell around her oval face. But I loved her nose the most: It was small and it turned upward when she smiled.

"I hate having to wear a scarf all day," Anahita said. "My hair gets so flat on top."

I peered at myself above her shoulder in the mirror. I turned sideways and saw my long hair looking a lot like a horse's tail, all bushy and sticking out with static.

"Maybe you should braid it," I said.

"No, then it gets frizzy."

"Do you think I should get a perm?" I pulled at my ponytail, hopelessly trying to tame the static.

"Didn't you say your mom wouldn't allow you to get a perm?" she asked.

"Oh, right." I dropped my hair.

Anahita stood up and said, "What do you want to do first: dance or watch a movie?"

"Let's dance first, to help me forget about our Religion teacher."

"Wouldn't our teachers just die if they knew we still do all the things we used to do before the revolution?" Anahita asked.

"If only. I wish I could go to class tomorrow and tell the teacher she'll burn in hell for trying to scare us all the time."

"Or that a student's father came to school to report having seen a strand of her hair sticking out of her scarf and that she should be fired for being an insolent Muslim woman."

"Oh, that's even better," I said. "Then she'll dangle from her own hair for eternity."

We both laughed hysterically.

"Okay, let's forget about all this and dance," she said.

Anahita and I loved to practice all manner of dancing together. It helped us forget about the Islamic Republic and the war. At least we were going through another phase where we weren't getting

regularly bombed, even though fighting raged along the border between Iran and Iraq.

The movie was at least four years old, but we were still crazy about *Grease*. We were convinced we could dance better than Olivia Newton-John and John Travolta.

The carpeting upstairs limited our wild dance moves, so we went downstairs to the living room to take advantage of the parquet floors. Just as it started to snow outside, Anahita popped the *Grease* soundtrack into the cassette player. We turned it on as loud as we could. Anahita and I danced and sang along to "We Go Together." After a series of swivels, spins, turns, and pivots, Anahita said, "Let's see if I can flip you over my head."

"What?"

"You know, like in the movie."

"Oh yes, let's try that," I said.

"Okay, here's what we're going to do," Anahita said. "I'll hold my hands out in front of me."

"I'll spin in front of you so we'll be back to front."

"Then I'll grab your hands from between my legs."

"And I'll grab them back," I said.

"I'll lift you up and flip you."

"I'll be lifted and I'll do a perfect flip!" I said.

It never occurred to us that there might be a problem, considering we weren't professional dancers, Anahita wasn't strong enough to flip me, and we weren't standing on a carpet or a pile of pillows, but on a hard floor.

So, we got into position. Anahita managed to lift me up quite a bit off the floor. Then everything happened very quickly. She let go of my hands as I was airborne, unable to flip me of course, and I landed on my head. Hard. Really, really hard. On parquet floor. Hard. I was so dazed that I couldn't move. My forehead rested on the floor while my arms were crumpled between my legs and my rear end stuck up midair.

Anahita threw herself on top of me, hit by a fit of mad giggles. She kept snorting, and between gasps asked, "Nioucha, are you okay?"

When I didn't answer, she tried to stop laughing but couldn't. She moved and managed to look at my expression by lifting the hair that had formed a curtain on both sides of my face.

Then more urgently she asked, "Seriously, are you hurt? Can you hear me?"

I rolled to my side and grabbed my head. Tears poured down my face from the shock of the pain and the absurdity of the whole situation. I saw her through my watery eyes, her expression frightened and slightly amused. I managed an "Ah-huh" to let her know I was still in there, somewhere.

I spent the rest of the afternoon nursing the bump on my head with a cold, wet towel and cursing *Grease* under my breath every time Anahita tried not to laugh.

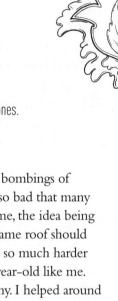

HIDING

1984

Gozashteha gozashte.
—Persian proverb

The past is past, or, let bygones be bygones.

I hadn't been going to school for a week. The bombings of Tehran had stepped up again. They'd gotten so bad that many parents had decided to keep their kids at home, the idea being that it was better we all stay together under the same roof should a bomb fall on us. It was spring, and that made it so much harder to be indoors all day, especially for an active 13-year-old like me. The only outside time we had was on our balcony. I helped around the house, played with two-year-old Nima, and spent hours on the phone with Anahita.

One day, I stood at the kitchen stove, mixing the barley soup we were taking to Aunt Minoo's. I was really looking forward to going because I hadn't left the house in three days.

Baba walked in, looking preoccupied as he put the kettle on to make tea.

Suddenly he blurted out, "Omid is back."

"Back from where?" I asked.

109

"Oh, I thought Maman told you …"

"Told me what?" I turned away from the stove to face him.

Baba took a deep breath.

"Aunt Minoo and Uncle Massoud tried to have Omid smuggled out of Iran, but he was caught at the border and arrested."

I burst into tears. Because, okay, despite his role as my childhood tormentor, he was still my cousin. My family. And ever since the day he gave me the Nutella, he'd shown me a new side of himself.

Baba put his arms around me and said, "He's home now. He's all right."

After I calmed down, he explained what had happened.

"Omid tried to leave, you know, like so many young boys have been lately, to avoid the war with Iraq," Baba said. "Aunt Minoo and Uncle Massoud paid a smuggler to get Omid out on foot."

"A smuggler?"

"Yes, it's pretty common now. This smuggler already helped a few of Omid's friends go to Turkey."

"Was Omid going to Turkey?"

"He was. Once there, the smuggler was going to give him a fake passport so he could go somewhere else if he wanted to."

"So what happened?" I asked.

"About a month ago, the smuggler called Uncle Massoud and said Omid had to leave that night."

"But why didn't he say goodbye? Why didn't anyone say anything about Omid being gone?"

"Because it had to be a secret. If too many people knew, the authorities might have somehow found out and the smuggler could have been arrested."

Holding Nima, Maman entered the kitchen. As soon as he saw me, he yelled, "Ya-yay! Ya-yay!"

That's what he called me, Ya-yay. I couldn't figure how Nioucha had become Ya-yay to him, but it was too cute to try to correct him.

Maman handed him to me so she could take over stirring the

soup. Nima nuzzled his head into my neck and left it there.

"Did you tell her?" Maman asked.

"I told her," Baba said.

"Baba, I'm confused. How did Omid get arrested if he was leaving?"

"Omid and about twelve other boys the smuggler was helping out reached the Turkish border a few days after they left Tehran. They walked at night along back roads and hid in the daytime. They were supposed to escape among a herd of goats, crawling under and between them. But all of a sudden, the border guards arrived with a van, dragged Omid and some of the others from the bushes they were hiding in, and threw them in jail. Only the smuggler and two of the boys weren't found."

"I'm sure there was a mole in the group," Maman said.

"Do you think?" I said.

"Of course," Maman said. "How else could the border guard know where the group was hiding?"

"You're right," Baba said. "Someone must have been paid by the authorities to track down these types of smugglers."

"Poor Omid," I said.

Maman and Baba exchanged glances.

"What?" I said.

Nima rose his head from his nestle and looked at me quizzically. I put him down and he began to take a few wobbly footsteps.

"Omid spent a month in solitary confinement, in a windowless cell," Baba said. "He was beaten every day. Uncle Massoud said his prison cell was so small he couldn't fully stretch his legs."

"Barbaric," Maman said, picking up Nima and propping him on her hip. "It's barbaric what they're doing to these young boys. Omid's just a kid."

I couldn't believe what I was hearing. Baba said that Aunt Minoo and Uncle Massoud initially had no idea Omid had been arrested. They were waiting to hear from him once he had arrived in Turkey,

which they had been told could take weeks. It wasn't until Omid's third week in prison that the smuggler contacted the families to tell them about the arrests. Uncle Massoud avoided Aunt Minoo for the rest of the day as he desperately tried to come up with a plan to rescue his son.

"I can't imagine what Massoud must have been through," Baba said, shaking his head.

"He should have told Minoo," Maman said.

"He did. Well, she coaxed it out of him."

"How?" I asked.

"She saw Massoud packing a bag to take with him to the Iranian border. She confronted him and he told her everything."

"Oh no!" Maman and I said.

Upon hearing the news, Aunt Minoo had fainted. After she regained consciousness, she became hysterical, screaming in anguish. Uncle Massoud gave her a sedative to calm her down. Sara took care of her mom while her father was away.

Uncle Massoud bought Omid's freedom with a bribe and brought him back home.

"Have you seen him yet?" I asked Baba.

"No, Omid and his dad arrived just a few hours ago," he said.

"Such a shame," Maman said.

I tried to picture Omid in solitary confinement, crouched in a cell that sounded like a cage. The image was so disturbing I had to shake it away.

We arrived at Aunt Minoo's house. Baba, Maman, and Nima went inside, but I hung back. On the drive over, I couldn't wait to see my cousin, but now I was nervous. Baba clasped Omid in his arms.

"I'm so happy to see you," Baba said.

"You too, Uncle," Omid said.

"Omid, we're so relieved you're home," Maman said.

"Me too," Omid said. "And look at this little guy!"

Nima squealed. Omid must have tickled him.

"Did Nioucha come?" Omid asked.

I felt my chest squeeze.

"Nioucha?" Baba called.

I had to go in. I slowly walked through the entrance and looked at my cousin.

I hardly recognized him. Instead of the round-faced boy with his unruly head of curly hair, I found a young man with a shaved head, sunken cheeks, and dark circles under his eyes. He had lost so much weight that he'd had to cinch his jeans up with a belt, the fabric hanging loosely around his thighs. He appeared lost in his polo shirt.

I stayed near the doorway, too overcome with the sight of him. I didn't know what to do. Omid noticed my hesitation and bowed his head, smiling sadly.

I took a step toward him. He opened his arms and said with a raspy voice, "Give me a hug, Nioucha."

It almost sounded like a plea. I fell into his arms. We held each other for a long time. In that moment, I remembered the last time I had felt this close to Omid.

~

All of Sara's friends and even some of Omid's friends had come to Sara's 16th birthday party. Sara's parents let her have the party in her bedroom, and they even bought her a brand-new stereo for the occasion. I danced with Sara and some of her friends. A few hours into the celebration, someone turned off all the lights in Sara's room. The only light came from the big stereo.

Omid put on some slow music. Everyone paired up and I was forced to stand in the corner. One of Sara's friends took a sweater out of her closet and covered the stereo to block the light. Now I had nothing to look at. It was so dark I couldn't find a path to the door to leave. I felt my way to the stereo and pulled the sweater off it. Everyone yelled, "*No!*" Startled, I turned around and saw that most couples were kissing. I couldn't believe my eyes. All I could think about were the many parents right downstairs, any of whom could have walked in on the party at anytime. I just stood there, embarrassed.

When the slow music ended, Omid put a Bee Gees cassette in and walked up to me.

"Are you okay?" he asked.

"Yes," I said. I wasn't used to Omid being nice to me. "Why?"

"You look a bit lonely, that's all. Do you want to dance?"

"With you?"

"Why not? Come on, I know how much you love to dance."

Omid and I danced to a few songs and then he returned to his own friends. That fun party of carefree dancing felt like a distant memory now.

~

"I'm so sorry about what they did to you," I whispered in Omid's chest.

"I'll be okay," Omid said. "You shouldn't worry about me."

After dinner, a few of us followed Omid to the upstairs sitting room. He had hardly spoken all night. The television was on at a very high volume and Omid sat very close to it, his right ear nearly pressed against the set. Nima, who was sitting in my lap, covered his ears with his hands.

I delivered him downstairs to Maman, and on my way back up, Sara told me, "Omid is deaf in one ear now."

"What do you mean 'deaf'?" I asked. "He's never had hearing problems before."

Sara cleared her throat and said, "They beat him every day and slapped his face so hard that he has a hard time hearing from his left ear. We hope it's temporary."

"Why did they beat him so much?"

"For deserting his country ..."

I felt a pang.

"Sara, what's going to happen now? Will he have to fight the war?"

"No," Sara said.

"How come?"

"It turns out, because Omid is the heir of our family, he does not have to fight."

"That's good news, right?"

"Sure, but all of Omid's friends left. It's not just about the fighting, you know. It's about leaving this situation, this regime."

I nodded.

Sara continued, "Omid still has to do his military service, but he can stay in Tehran for that. He won't be anywhere near the fighting."

"What a relief," I said.

But I worried about Omid. Would he ever recover from what happened to him? Would our country ever recover from this war?

LOVE

1984

Rassme ashegh nist ba yek del do delbar dashtan.

—Ghaani Shirazi, Persian poet

It is not the lover's way to have two sweethearts with one heart.

"Sara," I said. "I am in big trouble! You have to help me!"

My cousin was in my bedroom with me as I babysat two-year-old Nima to help Maman while she taught.

"What's going on?" she asked.

I hesitated before answering, but then blurted it all out.

"Okay, this girl Mitra at school found out I had a boyfriend— well, you know, ex-boyfriend now—and told her mom about it and so her mom came to school today and told me I was too young to have a boyfriend. She said she's going to come to my house tonight to discuss this with my parents because they have a right to know what their daughter is doing."

"Slow down, Nioucha," Sara said.

I took a deep breath.

"That Mitra," I said. "I hate her."

"Is she your friend?" Sara asked.

"Mitra? No way. She's one of these idiots who think everything the regime does is awesome."

I dropped my head in my palms and said, "Maman is going to be furious." Then I realized an even more terrifying truth, "Baba will kill me when he finds out I had a boyfriend."

"Are you sure this woman is coming tonight?"

"I don't know! She gave me a lecture about being a good Iranian girl and that having a boyfriend is totally out of the question. She said she felt it was her responsibility to come talk to them."

I felt desperate. Mitra had eavesdropped on Anahita and me talking about my breakup with Arya. She turned around and said, "Only immoral girls have boyfriends."

"You're just jealous!" I said.

She raised her eyebrows and said, "You have no idea what kind of trouble you have gotten yourself into."

And she walked away. I wanted to yell after her, "There's nothing to say now! I broke up with him!" but I didn't want to give her the satisfaction.

Though I brushed off her outburst, I still felt uneasy. I wasn't sure what she might do with this information about me. But I would never have guessed that she would run home and tell her mom. And that the mom would actually take time out of her day to come to my school, find me, and tell me she was coming over to my house to talk to my parents.

"I think your mom should hear this from you before a stranger comes over and tells it to her," Sara said.

I thought about this for a minute. The truth was, I didn't want her to find out at all.

"Maybe Mitra's mom won't come over after all," I said. "Maybe she was just bluffing."

Sara shook her head and didn't answer. Finally she said, "I'll stay here with you when you tell her."

I nodded. Maman had about 10 minutes before starting her class. Sara brought her into my room and told her I had something to say.

"What is it?" Maman asked. "Is everything all right?"

I swallowed hard. I couldn't find the right words and couldn't bring myself to look into her eyes. Sara put her hand on my shoulder, and when she did, I muttered an abbreviated version of the story.

At first, Maman blinked a few times and looked from me to Sara. Then a dark shadow landed on her face and she erupted in the angriest voice she could muster without waking up Nima: "*You* had a *boyfriend*? At *thirteen*?"

"Yes."

"Is this why you were always on the telephone?"

"Yes."

"You wait until your dad hears about this," she said.

"Wait, no, Maman, please don't tell Baba! Please, I'm begging you! He'll kill me!"

"Of course I'm going to tell him. What, you expect me to lie to him for you?"

"No, don't lie; just don't tell him, that's all. Anyway it's over now, so why …"

Maman didn't let me finish. She inhaled deeply and rose from the bed.

"I have to go teach my class now. We'll discuss this later."

When she was gone, I collapsed back in my chair and said, "Sara, please stay here tonight. If you're here, maybe Baba won't get too mad."

"Of course I'll stay. For now I'll take Nima to the park to give you some time to figure out what you're going to say to your father."

Sara and Anahita had been my only confidantes during this time. Sara had always told me about her dating stories, so it had been natural and fun to talk to her about my first boyfriend.

When Sara took Nima to the park, I pulled out my diary from the back of my desk drawer. I'd started this diary so I could remember the details of my first encounters with Arya. I leafed through the pages, pausing here and there to read an entry.

CHAPTER 10

Day 1

*I am officially Arya's girlfriend. That's why I am calling this
Day 1. I am so happy.*

*Adidas Boy (that's what I've been calling him, because he has
the nicest pair of white and navy sneakers I've ever seen—I want
his shoes) finally found the courage to hand me a note with his
phone number on it.*

*I've seen him almost every day for the last three months on my
way to school with Anahita. But because of the constant patrols of
the Black Crows, Anahita and I were beginning to wonder if he'd
ever make a move. (How come there are so many middle schools
and high schools in my neighborhood? The stupid regime doesn't
want any young boys and girls to even talk to each other, let alone
anything else. So we always have to be extra careful because the
Zeinab have arrested so many teenagers lately, saying they're having un-Islamic relations.)*

*Anyway, Arya was very careful when he handed me the note.
Actually, that's a lie. He didn't hand it to me; he sort of threw it in
my general direction. My heart was in my mouth when I picked
up his piece of paper. I stuck it in my pocket and waited until I
was at school to read it.*

*When we were on the playground, Anahita and I read the mes-
sage. It said:*

"My name is Arya. Here's my telephone number: 68 42 41."

*He's so cute. And I'm pretty sure he splashed men's cologne on
the page. Anahita thinks it's Drakkar Noir.*

*Every morning has been so exciting, waiting to see him at the
end of my street. He is always with a friend, and they wait there
until Anahita and I catch up with them. Then they start walking a
few feet ahead of us, turning around every minute to make sure we
were still there.*

Adidas Boy—wait, I should call him Arya now—always looks

right at me and smiles. He has dimples. They're so adorable, sink-
ing in his handsome long face. And he has these amazing hazel
eyes; they're huge too. His eyes seem to laugh when he looks at
me. I told Anahita the first day we saw him in the street that I
had a big crush on him.

This afternoon, I called Arya from Anahita's house. We both sat
on her bed and she glued her ear to the receiver so she could hear.
He picked up on the first ring. He had a powerful, deep voice and
I almost hung up because I was so nervous. I asked, "Is this
Arya?" He said, "Yes." I told him I was the girl of the note.

He said, "I know who you are."

Anahita and I giggled like mad.

"Is somebody there with you?" he asked.

"No, it's just me," I said.

Then Anahita shook me so we'd stop acting stupid.

"What's your name?" he asked.

"Nioucha."

"That's a pretty name, as pretty as you are."

I wondered through the phone if he could tell how hot my
face grew.

"Will you be my girlfriend, Nioucha?"

"Sure," I said.

Day 3

I talked to Arya for two hours yesterday and today. He told me
he is in 11th grade and he is 16 years old. I'm only 13 and in
eighth grade. Wow, I have an older boyfriend. He told me his
mother is pregnant, which is crazy because his eldest brother is 20.

He told me a funny story. His brother wanted to talk to his girl-
friend, but Arya lied and told him the telephone company had
come to their building to say the lines were out of service. And the
brother believed him. He left to use a pay phone at the end of their

street. Arya said he wanted the phone all to himself so he could speak to me as much as he wanted to.

I called Anahita afterward and told her everything.

Day 6

I really like him. He laughs through his nose. I told him I like his laugh, so for the rest of our talk, he kept laughing.

Maman thinks I am on the phone with Anahita. She'd probably have a fit if she knew I was talking to a boy.

Day 10

I finally told Arya that I am half French and half Iranian, and that I lived in Pittsburgh when I was little. He flipped out. He thought this was the coolest thing. Everyone usually has the same reaction as he does, and I always get irritated with their response. I just want to be ordinary …

"How did your parents choose Pittsburgh?" he asked.

"Because one of Maman's relatives lived there and recommended it to them. We lived in Pittsburgh for three years, long enough for Baba to get his master's degree in political science," I explained.

I usually try not to tell people that I have a weird background because as soon they know, they ask me so many questions. Yes, my mom is French. Yes, my parents met at university. Yes, they moved us to Pittsburgh for a few years. Yes, they moved us to Tehran afterward. I think what annoys me the most is when people say, "Oh can you please say something in French?" Why can't they just leave me alone? Of course, Arya did it too.

"What do you want me to say?" I asked.

"Oh, say something, anything. French is such a beautiful language."

I know it is, I wanted to say, I speak it every day at home.

So, in French I said to him, "I'm really tired of this conversation."

"What does it mean?" he asked.

"It means I really like talking to you," I lied.

He was so happy when I said that.

Then he asked if my half Frenchness is why I have green eyes and fair skin. I get this question all the time too. Everybody thinks I get my eye color from Maman's side. I don't understand this automatic assumption, because there are lots of pale, blue- and green-eyed Iranians.

I explained to him that the green eyes come from Baba's side of the family. That my Agha Jan and several of my aunts and uncles also have green eyes. That my own Maman has blue eyes, and aside from having her fair skin, I don't look like her. And so on, and blah blah, so forth. I should be used to all these explanations by now, but I am not. The reality is, I just want to be like all the other kids my age. Is that too much to ask? Anahita is the only person I feel totally comfortable with because she's mixed too. We call each other mutants.

Day 24

Arya stopped right in front of me. When I walked past him, he gave me this funny look and whispered, "Why didn't you call me yesterday? I missed you."

I whispered back, "I was waiting for you to call." But that is where our conversation ended. I saw the green jeep of the Zeinab at Vanak Square and moved quickly away from him, keeping my head down. Anahita walked even faster.

In the afternoon he called and said he is always the one calling and for once when he didn't (that was yesterday), I didn't either and that was a test to see how much I care about him. I said I was sorry. I guess I've gotten used to him calling me. But what is the

big deal? Why couldn't he just call me? Why does he have to test me? He's acting like a baby.

Day 30

I met Arya at a coffee shop today. We had to sit at different tables, of course, but he sat facing me, so that wasn't too bad. I was drinking my café glacé, but I was so excited that I don't remember even tasting it. Usually I love having one of these coffees. It was so cool to see him sitting in front of me. We're always on the phone or we just see each other on the street. Every time I looked at him, I felt my heart pounding. He just stared and smiled at me the whole time.

After a while, I got scared the Zeinab would raid the coffee shop. I noticed a few people in the shop looking at us, wondering why we were sitting alone. So I finished my drink quickly and left without looking at him. He left too and he sort of walked me home, but to be safe, he stayed a few feet behind me. He is so sweet.

Day 38

The Zeinab arrested Arya's brother and his girlfriend. His family has no idea where they've taken him. I can't even imagine what they must be going through. They're probably terrified. All the brother was doing was having a conversation with his girlfriend at a public park. They were sitting on benches facing each other. But wait, that's exactly what Arya and I had done at the coffee shop. I don't even want to think what could have happened to us. Anyway, even though they were being super careful (Arya walked around the area acting as their watchdog), they've been taken in.

So here's what Arya told me: The Zeinab (I hate them) were

cruising through the park on foot, saw them talking (oohh, talking), and bolted toward them. Arya quickly nudged his brother and they started walking away together. But one of the Zeinab guys snatched the brother's arm, while another stood over the girlfriend. They started asking the couple if they had a relationship. Of course, they both said no. But the Zeinab didn't believe them. They put them in the back of the jeep and took off.

Arya is completely freaked out. I'm worried—and pissed. Since when is it a crime for a boy and girl to speak to one another?

Day 39

I feel horrible for Arya and his family. I didn't see him on my way to school this morning. I called him as soon as Maman started her classes and he said he couldn't sleep all night, but then he did fall asleep and ended up being late for school. I tried to tell him about silly things that happened in class, just to distract him, but it didn't really work. He sounds really sad.

Day 40

The Zeinab released Arya's brother. They kept him for two whole days. They lashed the poor guy 80 times on his back. They said he shouldn't have been talking in public to a woman who wasn't a relative. I've heard of this sort of thing happening to lots of people, but I didn't know any of them. All right, so I've never actually met the brother, but still. This is so unbelievable.

The good thing is, they didn't do anything to the girl. They just gave her a scare and then told her she could go. Arya told me his family is so upset. His poor pregnant mother got sick when she saw her son's back (apparently, it's a real mess, all swollen with giant red gashes).

Arya was so angry that he kept raising his voice when he

*spoke to me. I think he feels guilty for not seeing the Zeinab
sooner. He keeps telling me he wants to attack the next Zeinab
he sees. I told him he was crazy, that they'd kill him. But Arya
said he didn't care. He said, "This situation is eating me up."*

I know how he feels. I hope his brother will be all right.

Day 42

Am I allowed to be annoyed with my boyfriend after he's been
through something so horrible? Probably not. But I can't help it.
And here's why: Arya asked what I had for dinner last night
and I told him my mom made beef Stroganoff. Now here's the
problem. I pronounced Stroganoff the French way, meaning I
kept the S silent and trilled the R, as it should be. But I should
have known better and pronounced it Es-to-rrro-ga-noof, the way
Iranians do.

Well, Arya just jumped on that and said several times, "Well,
listen to you, Ms. France, with your French pronunciations. Aren't
you just too classy and French for us?" Then he started doing
what I hate the most. He made these really silly mock attempts
at imitating my Stroganoff pronunciation. Over and over again.
I should have hung up on him.

People are always teasing me for saying French words the right
way. I should never make the mistake of pronouncing the names of
French actors, writers, or singers properly. Otherwise, they imitate
me, using regular Persian words that they try to pronounce with
French accents. They make these strange sounds that come from the
backs of their throats, trying to make R sounds. Because of this, I
decided to blend in and say words the Iranian way. But sometimes
I slip. Like now, with Arya.

Eventually he noticed that I wasn't saying anything or laughing
with him, so he said, "Are you still there?"

"Yep," I said. But I still didn't say another word.

Finally he said, "I'm sorry, Nioucha, I love your French accent."
"Too late," I said. "I have to go study now."

Day 50

So Anahita thought it would be a good idea for me to have
my legs waxed. She thinks that now that I have a boyfriend, I
shouldn't have hairy legs. And I said to her, "Who cares about my
legs? I'm always wearing jeans anyway." But she insisted, saying
I'll feel cleaner and more beautiful.

She's been all into getting fancy haircuts and clothes lately. Last
week, she got a pair of leather pants. I have to admit they were
pretty nice, but where is she going to wear them? We always have
to be in uniform and wear our scarves in public and at school. Plus
people aren't having too many parties these days, so we really don't
have a place to wear fancy clothes.

Anyway, back to my legs. Anahita managed to drag me to the
high-class beauty salon she's been going to on Gandhi Street. The
wax lady, a large woman with hennaed hair, came toward us and
motioned for us to follow her.

She showed us into a small room, said, "Take off your pants
and lie down," and left us.

Anahita did as she was told. She hopped on what appeared to be
a massage table covered with a sheet, while I hovered near the door.

A bathroom to the right of the door had only a shower, no sink
or toilet. Near the bed were the waxing items in a three-tiered
metal cart on wheels. The top shelf had the container of hot wax
and several bottles of liquids. The second and third shelves had
strips of white fabric and white towels.

The wax lady returned and without saying a word, began to rub
Anahita's legs to inspect the length of the hair. She bent Anahita's
left leg at a 45-degree angle, and smeared hot wax from the top
of her knee to her ankle. She then took a long rectangular piece of

127

fabric, pressed it down hard on Anahita's leg, and in one swift motion, pulled it off. I gasped.

I was sure Anahita's skin must have come off. But no. Her skin was intact and now bright pink. The wax lady continued her work on both legs, and not once did Anahita wince from the pain.

"You're done. Now go wash your legs," she ordered Anahita. Then to me, "It's your turn. Take off your pants."

I hesitated.

"Do you want to get your legs waxed or not?" she asked.

I nodded.

"Well, what are you waiting for?"

I took a deep breath, took my clothes off, and hopped on the bed. Anahita returned fully clothed and gave me a reassuring look.

The wax lady inspected my legs, running her rough hands up and down my shin. She said, "Never shaved before. Not that hairy. This will be easy. The hair will come right out."

And with that, she took the stick balanced on the container, dipped it, and put the wax to my leg. As soon as the hot liquid hit my leg I wanted to scream and run out the door. Instead, I leaned back like Anahita had just done and pretended like none of this was bothering me.

When the wax lady began rubbing the fabric on my leg, I felt panicky. Then she ripped the wax off and I howled in pain. The wax lady grabbed my hand and put it where the hair had come off. She said, "Press hard, press hard, the pain will go in a second."

After the initial pain was over, I glared at Anahita and said, "You lied. This is the most painful thing I've ever experienced."

"It's not that bad; you're exaggerating."

When another layer of wax was about to be spread on my leg, I screamed, "No, no, we're done here. I want to take my hairy legs home."

The wax lady moved my hands and continued to do her work as if she hadn't heard me. I whimpered for the next 15 minutes until she had done both sides of my legs.

All the way home I didn't speak to Anahita.

Day 55

The bombings have been pretty bad lately. Anahita and I skipped school so that we could stay close to home. Baba jokes that if a bomb falls on our house, it's better that we're all there so we can die together. I agree. My worst nightmare is that something bad will happen to one or two of us but that the rest will survive.

In other news, Aunt Minoo returned last week from her trip to America. She brought me lots of presents, including a Michael Jackson T-shirt. I love him. I guess she hasn't noticed how much I've grown lately. I mean the horizontal way, not so much verti- cally. She must not have seen that suddenly, out of nowhere, these huge breasts popped out. Anahita says she's jealous of my big boobs, but all I want is to hide them under big clothes. I actually love having to wear the Islamic robe in public now because nobody notices my chest. Well, anyway, I can put the T-shirt on, but Michael's face is distorted beyond recognition.

I think I'll give the T-shirt to Arya. He invited me over to his house for the first time. He says his parents will be at work, but that his brother and sister will be there. I guess the fact that his parents won't be home will make me feel less embarrassed for going over to a boy's house. Iranian girls are not supposed to have boyfriends, and sometimes I feel like a bad girl for having one. Plus, I'm only 13. Most of the older girls I know hang out with boys but they always lie and pretend to be pure and virtu- ous. Right.

Day 57

I met Arya's brother and sister. His sister is my age. She is nice but really shy. Or maybe she doesn't think her brother's girlfriend should come over to their house. Who knows?

When I took off my scarf, Arya kept saying things about my long light brown hair. How strange that I never even realized that he hadn't seen me without my scarf and robe on.

We all sat in their living room, drinking from cans of imported Coca-Cola and listening to the Thriller *album. Their apartment is a bit small, but nice and clean.*

Arya loved the Michael Jackson T-shirt. I brought some American bubble gum too. That always makes me popular because gum from other countries is expensive, and Iranian gum loses its flavor after two chews.

I wanted to ask Arya's brother about his arrest but decided not to. Arya had told me his brother's back was healing okay but that he refuses to talk about what happened.

I left after an hour. Arya walked me down the stairs and gave me a hug for the T-shirt.

Day 82

My hand is shaking so hard I can't keep my pen in my hand. I've been like this for a few hours now. I wish I could stay this giddy forever.

He kissed me today. In his bedroom.

I went over to his apartment after school; he was alone. We hung out in the living room for a bit, and then he said he wanted to show me his AC/DC poster in his bedroom (he shares it with his brother). The room was very tidy, and it had two dressers along one wall and a large balcony window along the other. Anyway, who cares about that?

Suddenly, Arya put his arm around my waist. I took a step back, I'm not sure why, but I guess being so close to him made me nervous. My heart was beating so fast I couldn't catch my breath. He moved away a little and said, "Nioucha, I really want to kiss you. Is that all right?"

I think I mumbled, "What?" But my blood sounded so loud in my ears that only he knows what actually came out of my mouth.

Again he asked, "Can I kiss you?"

I had no idea what to say. I wanted to kiss him, but instead of answering or nodding, I started to giggle. I couldn't help it. He was so close that the smell of his aftershave made me dizzy. I love his smell. By the way, Anahita was right: It IS Drakkar Noir. We went to a perfume shop and asked to get a sample of it and bingo. There's Arya in the bottle.

"What's so funny?" he asked. "Are you nervous? You shouldn't be. I like you a lot, Nioucha."

I felt tingly all over. His hazel eyes were even more beautiful up close. I could see green- and honey-colored specks in them. I started to feel less giggly. With his hands behind his back, he leaned in and gave me a peck on the lips. It was so quick I didn't have time to react—or respond. It was all so awkward and delicious at the same time. It's hard to explain.

Anyway, when he tried to kiss me again, I started to giggle. He asked, "Nioucha, do you know how to kiss?"

"Of course I know how to kiss," I blurted.

But I didn't. I didn't know how to kiss. How would I? I've never kissed a boy before. Why would he think I'd automatically know how to kiss him? Of course I've seen plenty of kissing in the movies but that was not helping me now.

So Arya decided to ignore my lie, and he started to give me a lesson on how to kiss. A lesson. How embarrassing and weird. He said stuff like the lips part and the bottom lip goes here and the upper lip goes there and something happens with the tongue.

Which was super awkward. And not at all romantic. But I suppose it had to be done. Because this time, when he leaned in, I didn't laugh. I let him kiss me. And it was perfect. And strange. And I think I blacked out a little.

Finally, I told him I had to go home.

"I'll walk you out," he said.

When I walked, it felt like I was walking through clouds. I know that sounds silly, but it's the best I can think of. Or I could say stupid stuff like I was walking on air, or my legs felt like cotton. Anyway, it was an amazing feeling. My first kiss.

I took a taxi from his street, went home, and immediately called Anahita and told her every single detail of my afternoon with Arya. She screamed when I got to the kissing part. She joked around and said that I now have become used goods. I told her to shut up, although the thought had occurred to me too. Right now though, I couldn't care less. My robe smells of Arya and I am completely intoxicated.

I shut my diary after Day 82 even though I had written through to the 182nd day, which was yesterday. I wanted to remember the first half of my entries, and not the second half, where I found out that Arya had another girlfriend while we'd been together. The phone rang and my present situation came crashing down, and I struggled to keep calm.

It was Arya again, and I told him I didn't want him to call my house anymore because he was a cheater and a liar. He said, "Let me explain, please!" But I hung up on him just like I had every day this week.

Baba came home after Maman had finished teaching and was preparing dinner. Sara and I stayed in my bedroom, but Nima ran on his chubby little legs to greet Baba. We heard them laughing together in the hall, Baba throwing Nima up in the air and kissing his cheeks. Then Baba went into the kitchen to say hello to Maman, and there he stayed for a long time. So long, in fact, that I began to believe I wasn't in as much trouble as I had anticipated.

But I couldn't have been more wrong. Baba knocked on my door, poked his head in to greet his niece, and without looking at me asked me to follow him to the living room. Maman was already there. She asked Sara to keep an eye on Nima playing with his toys in the TV room. What happened next became a blur. Baba was so angry and lectured me for so long that I couldn't keep listening.

I only remember him saying, "You think just because a boy wears fancy jeans and sneakers that he is a good guy? That he is worthy of you? Of course we know you'll have a boyfriend someday but you're still too young to have one now. You can't be too careful under this regime. What if the two of you had been arrested by the crazy authorities? You can't be seen in public with a man who isn't related to you. Has that not become clear to you by now?"

I thought it pointless to explain that I had never walked side by side with him in public, although I had seen him in the streets and the coffee shop. We had been so careful, and obviously nothing bad had happened.

I mostly held my head down while Baba scolded me. The few times I looked up, I noticed he was staring straight ahead and speaking through clenched lips. Maman didn't say a word. In the end, Baba told me I couldn't have any contact with my so-called boyfriend anymore and that I was grounded for two months. I wasn't allowed to use the phone (not even to answer it when it rang), I had to come straight home after school, and I couldn't go out with any of my friends.

"Now when did this woman say she was coming?" Baba asked.

"She said she'd stop by in the evening," I said.

But she never came. If Sara hadn't encouraged me to say something, my parents would never have found out about any of this. When I pointed this out to Sara she simply responded, "Things

always happen for a reason." I thought about this and I realized that in a way, I was relieved for the truth to have come out. It had been a struggle to drag the phone from the TV room to my bedroom without making anyone suspicious, and I had felt horrible lying to Maman when I went to his house.

I took Baba's punishment in stride, thinking it was only fair after I had deceived them this way. My parents just wanted me to be honest with them, and I felt guilty that I'd betrayed their trust. Besides, the second half of my diary contained not-so-flattering news about Arya. So I can't say that I was devastated at the prospect of never speaking to him again.

What bad luck for me that Mitra overheard my conversation with Anahita just a couple of days after I broke up with Arya. When Mitra threatened to bring her mother over to my house, I had been alternating between laughter and anger over the fact that just two days before, I had discovered that Arya had another girlfriend. How did I find out? Anahita and I saw him talking to Maryam, our land-lord's daughter, at the coffee shop where I'd met Arya once. Anahita and I loved that place and we went there all the time to have delicious café glacés.

Before we entered, we saw them sitting at a table together. They'd obviously been bolder than I had been. Maryam was all smiles and silly-looking giggles. I couldn't believe my eyes.

"What should we do?" Anahita had asked.

"Nothing, we wait across the street to see what happens."

Arya left before Maryam did. Anahita and I hid behind a car so he wouldn't see us, then quickly made our way to the coffee shop. We greeted Maryam, acting all surprised to run into her.

"Were you with that guy who just walked out?" I asked her.

She smiled and said, "Yes, that was my boyfriend. Why? Do you know him?"

I plastered a stiff smile on my face and said, "Well, that's funny because he's my boyfriend too."

"What are you talking about?" Maryam asked.

"Yeah, I've been talking to him for about six months now," I said.

"Arya's been my boyfriend for two years," Maryam said. "I can't believe he'd do this to me!"

She pushed back her chair and rose from her seat. Without saying another word, she snatched her purse and ran outside.

Anahita and I looked at each other and followed Maryam. We watched as she caught up with Arya a block away and began to sob. Her whole body shook while Arya looked around nervously. Maryam seemed to have lost all self-respect; we could see passersby stopping and watching her. Arya leaned his head down, said something, then walked away and jumped into a taxi. Maryam actually screamed and ran after him, unable to grab him as the car slipped away.

That's when I took Anahita's arm and said, "I think we should go."

We walked in silence for a while, and then we erupted in a fit of uncontrollable laughter. There was something so pathetic and humiliating about Maryam's behavior that I promised myself I'd never show that kind of desperation to Arya or to any other man.

I decided right then that I'd never speak to him again, not even to explain why I didn't want to speak to him again. He didn't deserve to know my reason. Besides, Maryam had probably taken care of that for me by telling him that I knew about their relationship. I didn't need to hear some lame explanation, especially after seeing how he left poor Maryam on the street like that.

When we finally calmed down, Anahita asked, "Are you okay?"

"I will be. That guy is a jerk!"

FURY

1986 (PART 2)

Dar nomidi basi omid ast
payane shabe siyah sepid ast
—Persian proverb

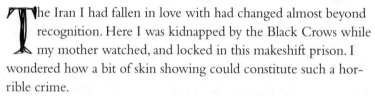

There is much hope in hopelessness;
for at the end of the dark night there is light

T he Iran I had fallen in love with had changed almost beyond
recognition. Here I was kidnapped by the Black Crows while
my mother watched, and locked in this makeshift prison. I
wondered how a bit of skin showing could constitute such a horrible crime.

Enraged, I felt ready to yell obscenities at the Black Crows. I put
my ear to the door, but I couldn't hear anything. This was the most
ridiculous situation. At fifteen, I was living the wrong life, the
wrong story, yet it was so real that it felt unreal. It was like a bad
joke or a bad movie. A nightmare. Any minute now, I would wake
up and none of this would exist.

My throat felt so dry I couldn't swallow. Blinking back tears,
I dug my nails into my fists until I drew blood. I stared at the
shapes I'd made in my palms, open-ended red parentheses. I
focused on the color changes, deep crimson to a bluish purple.
It was almost pretty.

I went back to the window and leaned my head against it. I closed my eyes.

I remembered Aunt Minoo recently asking Baba, "Brother, why are you staying here?"

Something in her tone made Baba look at her for a long time. Finally he had said, "But Iran is my home, Minoo."

"It's not hers," Aunt Minoo said. "You have a chance to start your lives over. Why aren't you taking it?"

Baba hadn't answered.

"Do you still think the regime is going to change? It won't! These ayatollahs are not going anywhere. But you can leave any-time you want."

"It's not that simple, is it?"

"Yes it is, brother. You don't have to feel guilty about us staying in Iran. Just think of your wife and kids."

Baba sighed and shook his head. After a long time, he picked up his book and left the room.

I knew why Aunt Minoo had confronted Baba so forcefully. Just four months ago she had spent four days in prison because she had been wearing nude panty hose. She had just jumped out of the car to buy Maman Bozorg a cake while Uncle Massoud waited for her in the car. The Zeinab swarmed in and arrested Aunt Minoo and several other women. They were taken away in a khaki jeep.

It happened so fast that Uncle Massoud had no time to react. All he could do was follow the jeep to see which prison they were tak-ing her to. He then hounded the guards for the next four days, beg-ging them for her release.

After she was freed, Aunt Minoo said she'd been in a communal room with 30 other women. There wasn't enough space for any-one to sit or lie down, so she'd been standing the whole time she was there.

Aunt Minoo had tried to laugh off her experience, saying that everyone in Tehran was getting harassed by the moral police all the

time, and what she'd endured was no better or worse than what any
other person had been through. But I could see that it had terrified
her. She had dark circles under her beautiful green eyes, and the few
times I'd been to her house lately, she'd been sleeping at odd hours
in the day.

At least my conditions in this room were nothing like what Aunt
Minoo had suffered through.

I heard someone coming toward my door. I checked my watch
and saw I'd been locked up for about three hours. It was still light
out. A key went into the lock and the door opened. I hid my hands
in my pockets. After enduring an array of indignant emotions rang-
ing from rage to despair to humiliation, I hadn't felt anything for
the last two hours. My body and mind entered a numb state, almost
catatonic. I had relentlessly eaten away the skin around my nails,
drawing blood from each finger.

Backseat Crow hovered in the doorway. I took a long look at her,
noticing for the first time a grotesque red scar running from the
corner of her right lip to her right temple, then disappearing under
her scarf. I felt a frightful satisfaction knowing that she had suffered
from the pain of that gruesome cut. She stared at me hard, seeing I
had detected her scar. She was ugly not because of the scar but
because of the loathing. It had turned her features into a permanent
scowl. It must be exhausting to hate so much. I was regaining my
senses, slipping out of my emotional paralysis. Just as quickly, I felt a
cold chill run down my back at the realization that this may not be
over. There was no telling what they would do to me.

She motioned for me to follow her out. Back in the living room,
Driver Crow sat at the table drinking tea. She didn't even look up.
I wanted to pour hot tea over her face for calling my mother a
whore. Backseat Crow led the way to the door of the apartment
and opened it.

"We better not see you again. If we do, you'll get a punishment
you'll never forget in your life. Now get out of here."

She pushed me out and slammed the door. For a second I stood there, not believing that I was free. But hearing movement from inside the apartment made me run down the stairs and outside onto the street so fast that I kept tripping over my feet. I ran so hard that I had side stitches, and black dots danced before my eyes. I had no idea where I was. I kept running even though drawing a breath felt like fire in my chest. Finally, I reached a busy intersection and flagged down a taxi. The driver was an old man.

"Can you please take me to Niloo Street? I have no money on me but my mother will pay you when we reach my house." I was breathless. My mouth was so dry that I retched when trying to swallow.

"Are you all right?"

I waited a few moments before answering, "The Women's Zeinab just released me. I really need to go home."

"Get in, get in, girl. I'll take you home. You're safe now. Don't worry about the money."

I gave him my address. He began a rant, more to himself than to me: "Look at what they've done to this country, look at what they're doing to our youth. How can they forgive themselves? Do they think they're pleasing God? What a joke."

I was shivering uncontrollably though it was still really hot out. My arms and fingers ached. I was thirsty, scared, outraged, and disgusted all rolled in one. The sight of my building was so comforting that I finally let myself cry.

"Sir, wait right here. I'll get your money."

"I don't want you to pay me. Just promise me you'll be more careful. Go home. I'll wait here until you're inside."

"Thank you so much!"

I rang the buzzer frantically. Looking anxious and worried, Maman and Baba peered out the open window. As soon as they saw me, they let out a sob. I ran inside the building and waved goodbye to the taxi driver. He honked his horn and drove off.

Maman and Baba met me in the stairwell and squeezed me in their arms.

"What did they do to our little girl? Did they hurt you? Are you hurt? Did they touch you? What did they do to you?" Maman saw my fingers and gasped in horror.

"No, they didn't do this. I bit my own fingers."

She wiped tears away. Baba took my head between his hands, kissed my forehead repeatedly, and suddenly released me, trying in vain to hide his tears. Maman fiercely clutched me to her chest. Baba put his arms around both of us. I never wanted to leave this safe cocoon.

We went inside. I told them everything, except what they said about Maman. Baba's face was distorted and his eyes were bulging the entire time I spoke. The veins in his neck stuck out. Maman kept caressing my face and hands. I sat between them on the living room sofa, drinking from a tall glass of cold water.

"Thank goodness you're okay, Nioucha. Thank goodness you're home," Maman said. "We were going crazy! I was losing my mind with worry! We didn't know where or how to look for you. We called every prison in Tehran to find you. We called the—" She stopped abruptly. "But you're home now and that's all that matters."

Nima, now four, wandered in and beamed at me. He had just woken up from his nap and followed our voices into the living room. He was so adorable, with his unruly hair and gorgeous chocolate-colored eyes.

He ran into my arms calling, "Ya-yay is home, Ya-yay is home!"

I squeezed him and buried my face in his little neck. I loved his smell. I loved how he curled himself into my body and clasped me in his arms.

"I love you, Ya-yay."

"I love you more, Nima."

I knew at that moment, our days in Iran would be numbered.

CHAPTER 12

DEPARTURE
1987

Kuh be kuh nemiresad, adam be adam miresad
—Persian proverb

Mountains don't meet, but people do

It was our last day in Iran, and I was sixteen years old. Aunt Minoo threw us a goodbye party and invited Christine and Anahita too. Maman Bozorg sat on the living room sofa and cried softly in her lace handkerchief. I couldn't even bear to look at her. Maman Bozorg waved me over. I sat next to her and put my head on her shoulder. She wrapped her arms around me and rocked me tenderly.

"I will miss you, my grandchild," she said. "Don't forget your grandmother who loves you very much."

"I will never forget you," I said. I tried to think of something else to say but I felt so lost. I cherished Maman Bozorg. I racked my brain to find a way to end her tears. Having thought I found one, I said, "I'll write you lots of letters."

"And I'll look forward to reading them," she said. "I'll write you letters too."

She kissed me on both cheeks and asked me to stop crying.

"Go eat something," she said. "You can't fly on an empty stomach."

I hovered near the dining room table, too overwhelmed to choose from all the food Aunt Minoo had prepared. My stomach was tied in a knot and I didn't think I could swallow anything.

Sara asked me to join her in her room. I put down my empty plate and followed her upstairs. Once inside, I saw that Omid and Anahita were already there. Sara handed me a $100 bill as a parting gift. I stood holding it awkwardly until Sara pulled me into her arms and whispered, "It's not going to be the same without you here, cousin. Who knows when we'll see each other again."

"I know," I mumbled.

"All right, Sara, don't hog her," Omid said. "It's my turn now."

I hugged Omid, dazed by the reality that I might never see them again.

"Don't fall in love with too many French boys," Omid said.

"I'll only be there for a few months," I said. "There won't be any time for that."

"You get to return to Pittsburgh," Sara said. "After all these years."

That had been my dream a long time ago. But now, leaving Tehran—the place with so many people and places I loved—filled me with dread.

"I can't believe you're leaving," Anahita said. "What will I do without you? You've been my best friend since we were only five years old."

"And you're mine. Who is going to be my best friend now?"

"Probably some American girl," Anahita said. "I'm already jealous of her."

"Don't worry," I said, hugging her. "I'll never love any friend as much as I love you, Anahita."

When we returned downstairs, I saw Anahita run outside. I followed her, but stopped when I saw her wiping her face. I went back inside, not wanting to encroach on her moment alone, but mostly because I felt terrible about her sadness. I longed for the hour when we'd have to go to the airport, to end this unbearable gloom.

And when it came, it all happened in a blur. I felt as though I was underwater and couldn't hear anything or speak properly. A wave of faces danced in front of me and I couldn't register last words and final embraces. We were leaving. It all felt so irreversibly final.

We arrived at the airport at 1:30 a.m. In the car, I sat next to Aunt Minoo, holding her hand tightly and saying goodbye to her in my heart. Omid rode in another car with Baba, Maman, and Nima. Our flight to Paris was scheduled at 6:00 a.m., but the airport personnel made passengers jump through so many obstacles that they always advised everyone to arrive at least four hours before their flights. By the time I was helping Baba and Omid with our luggage, the sadness had lifted and I was preparing for war with the nightmarish airport security.

The terminal was crowded and chaotic. We said our goodbyes without breaking down. There was too much tension to give in to the emotion. Maman pushed Nima in his stroller while I handled the cart loaded with the four large suitcases that contained our belongings.

We stood in line for passport control for about 30 minutes. Next came baggage control. When it was our turn, I pushed the cart toward a man who was waving us over. I'd been eyeing him for the last 45 minutes. He seemed the worst of the bunch.

"How many suitcases do you have?" he asked.

"Four," I said.

"Put them all up here." He motioned to the counter he stood behind.

Maman and I struggled to lift the heavy suitcases.

"Come on, hurry up!" he yelled.

When we were done, he said, "Open them! What are you waiting for?"

He went to the first suitcase, which had most of Nima's and my clothes. He flipped its contents onto the lid and proceeded to pick every item, shake it, and throw it back in. When he got to a bag of pistachios, he ripped the bag open, and spilled it onto an empty part of the counter. After he was certain nothing was hidden in there, he dumped the pistachios into a trash can.

"I'm done with this one. Now close it," he ordered.

Maman and I struggled to do so but everything had been thrown back in so haphazardly that we couldn't get the suitcase to close. This made our baggage guy impatient. He grabbed the troublesome suitcase and pushed it out of his way so he could get to the next one.

A passenger seeing our nervous efforts came by and helped us. He did the same when we were told to take care of the second and third suitcases.

"Why are you taking this out of the country!" the baggage guy screamed, bringing our attention back to him. He was going through the last suitcase.

"It's just an old *kilim* that the kids are attached to," Maman said.

"It's an antique," he said and shoved it in Maman's hands. "You're not allowed to take this."

"But what am I supposed to do with it?"

"Do you have someone still waiting in the terminal?"

Maman nodded.

"Go give it to them," he said. "And while you're at it, return these silver trays too. They look too valuable to leave the country."

Maman asked me to go find Baba and give him these confiscated items. I waited until the baggage guy was done humiliating us, and then went through the throngs of travelers to find Baba, who wasn't coming with us. He had to stay behind to wrap up his work. He said he'd be joining us soon, but I still hated having to say goodbye to him. He had said he'd wait until our flight took off in case something unpredictable happened. I couldn't join him in the terminal because I'd already been through passport control. I saw him outside smoking with Aunt Minoo. Luckily, Omid saw me wave frantically through the glass partition. Baba ran up to me and I told him what had happened. I climbed on a chair to hand him the kilim and silver trays.

"They're worried about an old rug and some banged-up trays?" he asked, looking up at me. "Unbelievable. How are your mother and Nima doing?"

"Maman is frustrated and Nima looks scared and sleepy."

"It'll be over soon," he said. "I'll wait right here."

He pressed my hand and I went back to find Maman waiting past the baggage control area. The next obstacle we had to go through was the body search. There were two separate lines for the women and men. They had set up small curtained cubicles for privacy. Maman and Nima went first. Then I went. Three women sat chatting on folding chairs, all wearing head-to-toe black chadors and white gloves. They ignored me for a few minutes. Then one of them reluctantly stood up in front of me.

"Are you hiding anything?" she asked.

"No."

"Spread your legs and arms for me."

She started with my hands, arms, and neck, and worked her way down to my breasts. She thoroughly searched all around them, especially when she reached the underwire of my bra. When she was satisfied, she got down on her knees and proceeded to feel her way around my private area. She cupped my butt and felt her way between my legs. I closed my eyes and willed myself to stay calm.

She got up and said, "Take off your scarf, open the top button of your robe, and undo your ponytail."

I did as I was told. With no scarf on, I suddenly felt naked standing in that shabby cubicle.

She saw my gold necklace, a simple chain with a small flower pendant, and my sapphire earrings. She grabbed my hands and saw the gold ring I wore on one of them.

"What makes you think you can take all this gold out?" she said.

I didn't answer. "Take off your gold chain. You can't leave with it."

"Fine," I said.

Maman and I had sold most of our gold. We knew we were limited in the amount of gold we could take with us, so we had settled on the jewelry that had sentimental value. The necklace I was forbidden to leave with, for instance, was one I had bought with my own allowance when I was 10 years old. I had worn it for the past six years. The number of gold pieces I had did not exceed the allowable quantity, I was certain, but this woman wanted to make a point.

I walked out and found Maman outside.

"They've told me I can't take my gold bracelets with me," Maman said. She handed me the bracelets Baba had given her when Nima was born.

"They said the same about my necklace."

"I've had enough of this," she said.

"Maman, I'll be right back."

And once more, I retraced my steps to find Baba. He wasn't surprised to see me again.

When he saw what I handed him he said, "I'll bring these when I leave. Tell your Maman not to worry, all right?

"I'll see you soon, Nioucha," he said with a broad smile. I waved to Omid and Aunt Minoo for the last time.

It was finally getting near the last stages before boarding the airplane. We sat resting in the waiting room of our gate as Nima slept in his stroller. Maman and I didn't have the energy to speak. About an hour before our flight, three men arrived at the gate and took their positions behind a desk. They asked passengers to form a line to have their passports checked and stamped.

"It's almost over," Maman said. She put her arm around my shoulder and gave it a little squeeze.

Dozens of people stood ahead of us. We heard the stamps banging against the table. Finally, Maman handed the man her French passport. Nima and I were still under the age of 18, and as such, we didn't have our own passports yet. The man took it from her and scrutinized it.

"Where's the visa?" he asked, flipping through the pages and looking confused.

Maman took the passport, turned to the page where our visas were registered, and pointed to it. The man checked it suspiciously, said something to his colleague standing next to him, and walked away from the gate, taking Maman's passport with him.

"What happened?" Maman asked.

The other man said brusquely, "Stand aside. You can't board the airplane."

"What?" we said.

"I said stand aside. You're in everybody's way."

Confused and irritated, we stepped away from the line. I felt as if my head was going to explode as I thought, "I hate you. I hate all of you. You are the reason we have to leave our home."

Maman said, "Nioucha, if they see the look on your face, they might not let us leave at all. We are at their mercy now, so please try to calm down."

Nima, who had woken up, began to cry from the tension and from the tone of our voices. Maman started pacing to quiet him down while I stood firm, with my arms crossed and "I hate you" chants emanating from every pore of my body, even though I honestly tried to calm down as Maman had asked.

Twenty-five minutes later, after everyone had boarded the airplane, the man reappeared with a new person in tow. They came up to Maman and said, "This is not a valid visa."

"What are you talking about?" I blurted.

Maman put her hand on my shoulder and asked them, "What's wrong with it? I obtained it from the French Embassy."

"It says here that you have two children," he said. Then pointing to me, "But she is clearly not a child. She doesn't have a valid visa."

"Of course she does," Maman said. "She is only sixteen years old and

doesn't have her own passport yet. But as you can see, she is on mine."

"It says here that she is an *enfant*," he continued. "An *enfant* means baby and she is not a baby. She can't get on that airplane."

"*Enfant*, sir, means child, not baby," Maman said. She was using her teacher voice. "As in both Nioucha and Nima are my children. It can also mean a small child, but when used in an official document such as a passport, it means a parent's child. It does not quantify an age."

Maman looked through her purse and pulled out my birth certificate. Pointing to my birth date, she said, "Do you see? She is sixteen and by law she is underage and my *child*. Is that clear now?"

The men looked at each other and turned their backs on us. I could barely bring myself to look at them or at Maman. I shook with anger and felt like a maniac ready to screech! I could see our Iran Air flight sitting outside the gate.

The waiting room sat empty. The men told us to wait a few minutes while they decided what to do. The four of them stepped away from us and had an intense conversation. Maman and I held our breaths. After what seemed like an eternity, one of them returned and said, "You can go." He stamped Maman's passport and gave it to her.

We ran to the airplane to begin our new lives. In freedom.

~

I stared at the pillow of white clouds under us, so peaceful and so removed from the troubles of the world. I felt the hatred and resentment for this regime gradually dissipate. If only life could be as simple as flying smoothly through a welcoming sky.

Nima was asleep, his curly head of hair leaning against my arm. His small feet dangled from the airplane seat. Maman sat on Nima's right and was nodding off.

As I pushed back tears, I wondered if Nima would remember his short life in Iran. After all, he was only five years old. What would he miss? His cousins? His canvas tent on the balcony where he played with his Lego bricks and Matchbox cars for hours?

I had forgotten so much of my life in Pittsburgh. I had only been five too when we moved to Iran. I had trouble figuring out whether my memories came from pictures or stories Maman had told me.

Would Nima remember the lies I told him during the bombings?

"What was that sound?" he would ask me.

"It's just fireworks, Nima," I'd say as I carried him down the stairs to the basement. He held on to fistfuls of my long hair, a soothing habit he'd had since he was an infant. Maman and Baba followed closely behind with the Dior bag and flashlights.

"Can we go see them, Nioucha?"

"No, Nima, it's best for us to stay here in the dark and play hide-and-seek with the neighbors."

I made sure I kept my voice low. I don't know why. Crazy though the idea was, on some gut level I guess I feared the Iraqis could hear me from miles above and target our building. *Ah, I hear a teenage girl's soft voice—let's bomb her building!*

Nima hadn't questioned me.

I began to think about our new lives in America. So much of my focus had been on getting ready to leave that I hadn't given much thought to our destination.

Worries about what awaited us began to creep into my head. Will I be able to make American friends? How long will it take for Baba to join us? What if he can't get out of Iran? Will I stand out like a strange foreigner at school? Will I remember enough of my English to get by?

I had no idea.

Nima had shifted in his sleep. He stretched out his little body across Maman and me. His head lay in my lap. I caressed his hair with one hand and laid the other across his torso. I felt his heartbeat and the rhythmic rise and fall of his small chest.

I remembered Maman Bozorg's last words: "Don't look back. Go to your new life but don't forget where you came from. And don't forget that you have a family here that loves you."

I will never forget.

AFTERWORD

Omid an ke zendeh bemani to ey vatan   chandan ke khak ra bovad-o bad ra bagha
Dar khak khofteh "homayoonfarat", vatan   Roozi ke majde to gardad ze no be pa

—Dr. Ezatollah Homayoonfar, poet and writer

I hope you last forever O fatherland   Just as earth and wind are eternal
Your homayoonfar is resting underground, fatherland   Until the day you will be born again

I'm sitting at my desk in my home near Washington, D.C. My two small kids circle around me, wondering when I'll be done on the computer so I can read them a story. They love stories. This one was written for them, and for you.

After Maman, Nima, and I left Iran, we began our lives in America. Baba joined us six months later. I can sum up our transition in one word: challenging. As recent immigrants, my family endured emotional ups and downs. Attending high school in Pittsburgh was one of the low points for me. For the first few months, I was that strange foreigner who nobody wanted to be friends with. I felt overwhelmed with my new life and so out of place.

Baba had a difficult time too, occasionally regretting our decision to move across the world from where he had such deep roots. He said he wanted to go back to Iran. Maman worked hard to keep us glued together when Baba and I thought our homesickness would break us apart. She carried a heavy load. Thankfully, Nima was blissfully young and happy in a world of *Teenage Mutant Ninja Turtles* and Nintendo games. When he entered first grade in our neighborhood school, he immediately found a group of friends.

We pulled through those tough times. Baba became a political science professor at a local university and Maman a French teacher at a private girls' school. Before long, I spoke with an American accent thanks to watching hours of sitcoms like *Family Ties* and *The Facts of Life*.

I was accepted at the University of Pittsburgh as an art history major. I made friends, graduated, worked, and traveled. I felt more and more integrated into American society and culture and loved the freedom to wear whatever I wanted, say whatever I wanted, and do whatever I wanted. Nobody bothered me. It was amazing.

After 11 years in America, Baba and I decided it was time to visit Iran. Maman still didn't think it was safe for Nima to go, so they didn't come with us. Before we left, I wrote to my cousin Sara to tell her we were coming to visit.

June 1998

Dearest Sara,

I can't wait to see you again. It's been so long!

Baba and I arrive in one month. We have an eight-hour lay-over in Amsterdam, so we'll be pretty tired by the time we land in Tehran.

I know that you and Aunt Minoo and Omid will be at the air-port, but please ask Maman Bozorg to wait for us at home. It's too late in the night and I don't want her to get sick on our account. I'm sure she'll be awake when we get to her house. I'm dying to see her, to see all of you. And I'm salivating just thinking about all of Maman Bozorg's delicious meals. I'm going to gain at least 10 pounds there and it'll be totally worth it.

Baba took the summer semester off from university so we could stretch our trip to three weeks. Do you know that he's been voted most popular professor again? It's the third year in a row!

My supervisor at the museum is pretty upset I'm taking so much leave, but they're trying to be understanding.

I'm sorry Maman and Nima are not coming. I know you all want to see them and I would love to have them in Tehran with us. But Maman doesn't want Nima to travel to Iran. She's terrified the government will force him to stay there and do his military service. Plus, she swore never to have to wear a scarf by force again. Believe

me, Baba and I tried to change her mind, but she won't have it.

Nima just finished his first year of college and moved back home from the dorms. He's going to the University of Pittsburgh like I did. I guess hearing me talking about my experiences at Pitt made him want to go there too. He's studying finance. I wish I had his brains! Getting a degree in art history didn't exactly open the door to many lucrative jobs, but I love it, even if I can hardly make ends meet living in New York.

By the way, remember my childhood friend, Anahita? Well, I haven't told her I'm coming to Iran yet. I wanted to surprise her. Did you know she named one of her daughters after me? It's hard to imagine her with two toddlers, even though I know she must be a wonderful mother. Speaking of mothers, Christine—Anahita's mom—will be so surprised to hear that Maman is still teaching French, although this time to Americans.

I'm counting down the days. Thanks for letting me know that the Iranian airport personnel are polite and civil now. At least we won't have to deal with that nonsense again.

Please let me know what you want me to bring from here. I am so excited!

> *Much love,*
> *Nioucha*

When Baba and I stepped off the airplane in Tehran, the smell of dust mingled with mountain mist hit me straight in my chest, bringing tears to my eyes. Oh how I missed my home. Aunt Minoo was waiting for us at the airport, with Sara, Omid, and Maman Bozorg. We all wept in each other's arms. It had been too long.

So much had changed. Maman Bozorg seemed smaller and less dynamic. She surrounded herself with the people she loved most. During that visit, she gently handed me the ring Agha Jan had given her on their wedding day. When I refused to take it because of the sentimental value it had for her, she said, "It's the only thing I have to give. Please accept it, my child." I wear it every day.

Aunt Minoo no longer lived in that big house I remembered so fondly. After her husband, Uncle Massoud, passed away, their son, Omid, had become a successful developer, building lavish condominiums on plots of land that his father's family owned. Aunt Minoo now lived in one of those condos, where she fulfilled her passion, becoming a popular interior decorator. She was as bubbly and sweet as ever. Sara now worked as a human resources manager as well as an English tutor. She took me to new trendy spots in Tehran, where I drank café glacés, shopped for jewelry, and met her friends. Omid married a wonderful woman he'd known since his teens.

As for Anahita, she was married and had two little girls. I called her the day after we arrived and told her I was there. She squealed into the phone and said she'd come pick me up immediately to bring me to her house. She and her husband had moved to a suburb of Tehran. Our lives were very different, but our love was as strong as ever. Nioucha, the younger of Anahita's two daughters, wrapped herself around me as though she'd known me her whole life.

Tehran itself had grown and expanded. There was construction all across the city: new highways, buildings, malls, restaurants, coffee shops, and parks. I didn't see the Komiteh anymore. My cousins told me they still patrolled the streets, but not as much as they had when I lived there.

I am so thankful for our lives in America. I have been blessed with many wonderful adventures and opportunities in my career in international affairs. My husband and I have a daughter and a son. Maman and Baba are regular visitors at our home, and whenever Nima can take a vacation from his financial analyst job in St. Louis, Missouri, he comes to see us.

But sometimes Iran still tugs at my heart. The smells, sounds, and colors of Tehran hit me at the most random times, and a sob bubbles up in me. For a moment, I wish I were in that vibrant city one more time, on my way to visit Maman Bozorg.

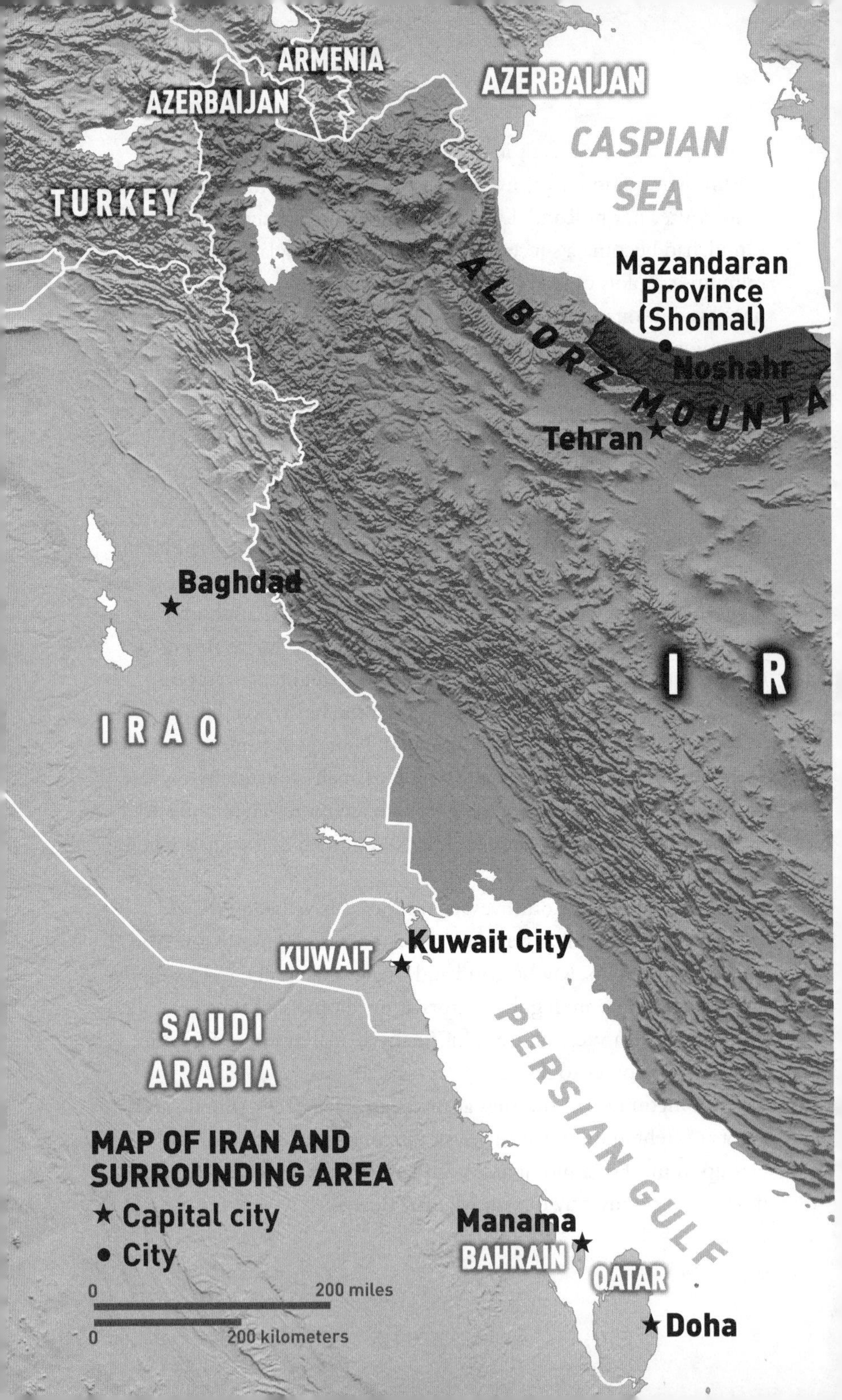

TURKEY

ARMENIA

AZERBAIJAN

AZERBAIJAN

CASPIAN SEA

Mazandaran Province (Shomal)

Noshahr

ALBORZ MOUNTA

Tehran ★

I R

Baghdad ★

IRAQ

Kuwait City

KUWAIT ★

PERSIAN GULF

SAUDI ARABIA

MAP OF IRAN AND SURROUNDING AREA

★ Capital city
● City

0 ——————— 200 miles

0 ——————— 200 kilometers

Manama
BAHRAIN ★

QATAR

★ Doha

UZBEKISTAN
TURKMENISTAN
Arctic Ocean
Atlantic Ocean
EUROPE
ASIA
Iran
AFRICA
Indian Ocean
Ashgabat
Mashhad
INS
A N
AFGHANISTAN
PAKISTAN
UNITED ARAB EMIRATES
OMAN

TIMELINE OF IRANIAN HISTORY

4200 B.C. — Iran's first city, Susa, is built.

552–486 B.C. — The Persian Empire is established and extends its rule from the Mediterranean Sea to what is now Pakistan.

330 B.C. — The Greeks conquer the Persian Empire.

260 B.C. — Nomads called Parni defeat the Greeks and take over in eastern Iran and a region of northeastern Iran known as Parthia.

A.D. 224 — The Sassanids come to power. They try to bring back Persian traditions and eliminate Greek influences. The Sassanids rule marks the last dynasty of the Persian Empire before Islam takes over.

A.D. 637–651 — The Arabs take over the Persian Empire. Persia becomes part of the Islamic Empire.

1501 — The shahs of Iran's first dynasty, the Safavids, begin their reign.

1921 — Reza Pahlavi, a Persian army officer, gains control of the country.

1935 — Reza Pahlavi renames Persia "Iran."

1941 — Reza Pahlavi's son, Mohammad Reza Pahlavi, becomes shah after Reza Pahlavi is removed by British and Soviet troops.

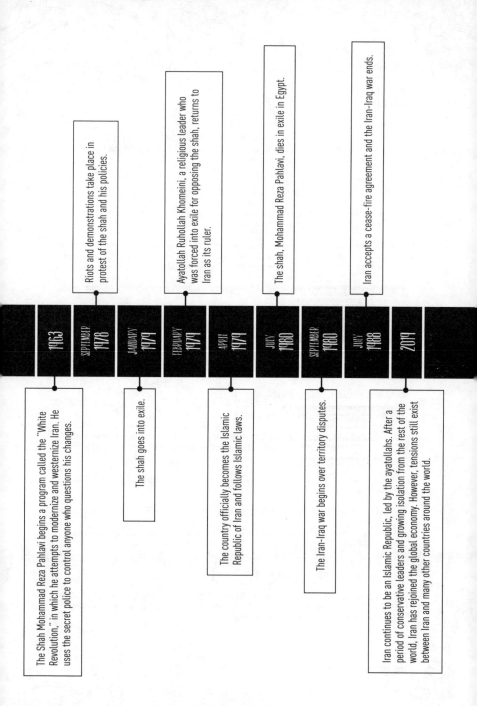

1963
The Shah Mohammad Reza Pahlavi begins a program called the "White Revolution," in which he attempts to modernize and westernize Iran. He uses the secret police to control anyone who questions his changes.

SEPTEMBER 1978
Riots and demonstrations take place in protest of the shah and his policies.

JANUARY 1979
The shah goes into exile.

FEBRUARY 1979
Ayatollah Ruhollah Khomeini, a religious leader who was forced into exile for opposing the shah, returns to Iran as its ruler.

APRIL 1979
The country officially becomes the Islamic Republic of Iran and follows Islamic laws.

JULY 1980
The shah, Mohammad Reza Pahlavi, dies in exile in Egypt.

SEPTEMBER 1980
The Iran-Iraq war begins over territory disputes.

JULY 1988
Iran accepts a cease-fire agreement and the Iran-Iraq war ends.

2019
Iran continues to be an Islamic Republic, led by the ayatollahs. After a period of conservative leaders and growing isolation from the rest of the world, Iran has rejoined the global economy. However, tensions still exist between Iran and many other countries around the world.

159

CREDITS

Photo Credits:
Cover: background pattern, David Curtis; woman, Suleyman Orcun Guler/EyeEm/Getty Images; author as a child, courtesy of the author; Flap: author photo, Lori Epstein/NG Staff; insert, all photos courtesy of the author, except Tehran cityscape, Michael Coyne/National Geographic Creative

Since 1888, the National Geographic Society has funded more than 12,000 research, exploration, and preservation projects around the world. The Society receives funds from National Geographic Partners, LLC, funded in part by your purchase. A portion of the proceeds from this book supports this vital work. To learn more, visit natgeo.com/info.

For more information, visit nationalgeographic.com, call 1-800-647-5463, or write to the following address:

National Geographic Partners
1145 17th Street N.W.
Washington, D.C. 20036-4688 U.S.A.

Visit us online at nationalgeographic.com/books

For librarians and teachers: ngchildrensbooks.org

More for kids from National Geographic: natgeokids.com

National Geographic Kids magazine inspires children to explore their world with fun yet educational articles on animals, science, nature, and more. Using fresh storytelling and amazing photography, Nat Geo Kids shows kids ages 6 to 14 the fascinating truth about the world—and why they should care. kids.nationalgeographic.com/subscribe

For information about special discounts for bulk purchases, please contact National Geographic Books Special Sales: specialsales@natgeo.com

For rights or permissions inquiries, please contact National Geographic Books Subsidiary Rights: bookrights@natgeo.com

National Geographic supports K–12 educators with ELA Common Core Resources. Visit natgeoed.org/commoncore for more information.

Hardcover ISBN: 978-1-4263-3366-8
Reinforced library binding ISBN: 978-1-4263-3367-5

The publisher would like to thank the following people for their work on this book: Priyanka Lamichhane, senior editor; Julide Dengel, art director and designer; Dawn McFadin, designer; Lori Epstein, photo director; Molly Reid, production editor; and Anne LeongSon and Gus Tello, design production assistants.

Printed in China
18/PPS/1